After-School Success

D0807384

Governors State University
Library
Hours:
Monday thru Thursday 8:30 to 10:30
Friday and Saturday 8:30 to 5:00
Sunday 1:00 to 5:00 (Fall and Winter Trimester Only)

DEMCO

After-School Success

Academic Enrichment
Strategies with Urban Youth

Anne Bouie

Foreword by
Lucy N. Friedman

TEACHERS
COLLEGE
PRESS

Teachers College
Columbia University
New York and London

Published by Teachers College Press, 1234 Amsterdam Avenue, New York, NY 10027

Library of Congress Cataloging-in-Publication Data

Bouie, Anne.
  After-school success : academic enrichment strategies with urban youth / Anne Bouie.
    p. cm.
  Includes bibliographical references and index.
  ISBN-13: 978-0-8077-4745-2 (pbk. : alk. paper)
  ISBN-10: 0-8077-4745-9 (pbk. : alk. paper)
  1. Project Interface (Oakland, Calif.) 2. After-school programs—California—
Oakland. 3. Urban youth—Education—California—Oakland. I. Title.
  LC34.5.C2B68 2007
  371.1909794'66—dc22

                                                                2006027324

ISBN-13:   ISBN-10:
978-0-8077-4745-2 (paper)   0-8077-4745-9 (paper)

Printed on acid-free paper

Manufactured in the United States of America

14 13 12 11 10 09 08 07   8 7 6 5 4 3 2 1

In appreciative memory of Evelyn Moliare, Edith Gottlieb, William Hunt, Jacqueline Haywood, Lewis B. Mayhew, James March, Gail Hamilton, Cornelia Bernard, Alberta Green, Don Duffy, Quincy Gainer, W. W. Gainer, and Charles E. Bouie.

Contents

Foreword

I T'S DIFFICULT to open a newspaper without reading about some aspect of the failings of public education. Children are graduating from high school unprepared to succeed in college—or worse, not graduating at all. *Time* magazine recently reported that nearly 1 in 3 students in the United States will not receive diplomas. The statistics are more frightening for young people of color: A staggering 50% never complete high school. In math and science in particular, U.S. performance is consistently below other western countries.

After-School Success is about how to turn these numbers around. While politicians seek to remedy the national education crisis through legislation—most notably with the No Child Left Behind Act—Dr. Anne Bouie presents a different strategy for change: using the assets in the community to build a positive, structured, and meaningful learning environment for students *after* school. In creating and leading the Project Interface math and science enrichment program, Dr. Bouie did more than teach kids; she gave them hope.

A program operating in the 1980s, Project Interface is an important predecessor to present-day after-school initiatives. She embraced students from nontraditional families, students from poor neighborhoods, students that claimed not to care about the Cs and Ds on their report cards. Then the entire community—family members, church leaders, college students, corporate volunteers, school principals, and local shopkeepers—was rallied toward the goal of improving kids' math and science skills. With so many caring people teaching, guiding, and believing that these young people could succeed, is it any wonder that they did?

This provides us with an inspiring model for building a quality program from the ground up. Imagine if every child in America was able to study with a scientist after school. Imagine them taking field trips to the park to study plants, building kites to learn physics, measuring the acidity of local rivers to put chemistry into context. Every day, students would stay late to learn from a new kind of teacher—perhaps a college student, corporate volunteer, or community leader—and their lives would be enriched for doing so. Young people would be able to set large goals for tomorrow because of small projects done after school today.

This is also the vision that guides The After-School Corporation (TASC), of which I am president, in New York City. Dr. Bouie states it well when she says that a facility that is full of caring adults and lacking supplies is an infinitely better environment for learning than a state-of-the-art facility in which no one believes the kids can succeed. The public needs to support the thousands of people across the country who will not accept failure in our schools. I am certain that the drop-out problem could be solved if young people believe they have the academic ability and sufficient opportunities to achieve academic success. The most important lesson kids can be taught is that it is indeed within their reach.

As the number of programs like Project Interface increase we must be careful, though, to maintain the high student expectations and employ the type of committed staff members that were PI's foundation. National organizations, such as the Afterschool Alliance, are working to promote excellence in after-school programs. Their "Lights on Afterschool" campaign raises awareness about the importance of after school. It helps us remember that after-school education is often the light to which children look forward at the end of *every* school day.

This reminds me of an Isaac Asimov quote that I dedicate to Dr. Bouie and everyone who was part of Project Interface: "There is a single light of science, and to brighten it anywhere is to brighten it everywhere." Their devotion effectively turned on the light for the kids in this program. If enough passionate people follow in their footsteps, our nation will once again shine.

Lucy N. Friedman
President
The After-School Corporation

The Interface Approach to Improving Student Engagement and Academic Achievement

> There is a principle which is a bar against all information, which is proof against all arguments and which cannot fail to keep a man in everlasting ignorance—that principle is contempt prior to investigation.
> —Herbert Spencer, ThinkExist.com Quotations Online

THIS HANDBOOK shares the efforts and results of Project Interface (PI), an after-school mathematics and science enrichment program for students in grades 7, 8, and 9. It was developed as a partnership between the Northern California Council of Black Professional Engineers (NCCBPE) and the Allen Temple Baptist Church in Oakland, California, to increase the number of African American youngsters prepared to pursue careers in math and science. For 7 consecutive years, PI students have outperformed comparable Oakland Public School students on the Comprehensive Test of Basic Skills (CTBS), and 60% of its graduates were enrolled in college preparatory classes as sophomores in high school. Staff members from a variety of backgrounds and experiences were effective in creating a nurturing learning environment for student achievement. Students showed significant and consistent academic achievement, and they transferred from middle school general math classes to mathematics and science classes that prepared them for entry into the high school classes they needed for college entrance. Parents were not only allies; they were also strong partners in the education and nurture of their children. Parents, children, and program staff were supported and strengthened by the commitment, involvement, and contributions of the immediate and larger community.

The first section is a thorough presentation of the genesis of the PI program philosophy, purpose, and initial partnerships, which led to the development of program goals and a structure for program design, implementation, and evaluation. The second section is comprised of the program-level steps we completed to prepare for successful student sessions, including staff and student recruitment, staff training, and curriculum design. The third section uses the direct experiences of participants in the PI program to give the reader a concrete sense of the most challenging circumstances facing children, parents, educators, and community members.

Chapter 1 describes the source and origins of the program's mission and guiding philosophy, stressing the importance of continuity and fit between a program and its creating organizations. The way in which Project Interface formed its identity may be helpful to practitioners who are in the process of defining a sense of purpose and direction and are examining different options, such as whether to focus on academics, social development, or other areas or to pursue a combination of goals. Appendix A includes initial checklists for partnership development (Figure A.1*) and program design (Figure A.2); Figure A.3 shows a chart of suggestions based on experiences at Project Interface that may be useful to policy makers and practitioners at local, state, or national levels to gain a broad understanding of potential roles to be played in the establishment of effective after-school programs.

Chapter 2 discusses our experiences in gaining entry and developing credibility and working partnerships with schools and community organizations. Simply gaining access to schools and students can prove to be a daunting challenge for many programs, particularly for those based in large cities with complex administrative structures and for those that attempt to engage with urban schools that are overwhelmed with daily calls from people who wish to help them. In addition to schools, potential partners might include churches, youth development centers, and other community-based organizations. Chapter 2 offers suggestions on the kinds of materials a program might wish to prepare and guidelines on how to frame presentations when approaching various audiences. PI student and parent contracts appear in Figures B.1 and B.2.

Chapter 3 provides examples of PI's experiences with community involvement, board development, fund-raising, program evaluation, and the use of quantitative and qualitative results. Project Interface could not have grown over the years without the nurture and involvement of the neighborhood and the larger community. We were fortunate to have an array of corporations, professional and civic societies, businesses, and individuals that contributed time, talent, and resources to the program. This chapter shows how we built those relationships. Appendix C includes a summary of PI's quantitative data (Figure C.1) and a chart of suggestions that practitioners may wish to consider in creating an effective program (Figure C.2).

Chapter 4 opens the second section and addresses program preparations through PI's development of an approach to student recruitment as a crucial and ongoing program component. Concerns about which students to recruit,

---

Editor's note: All the figures cited in this work are found in the Appendixes section.

at which grade levels, and at what times of the year can be challenging for many programs. This chapter includes reflections from our experiences in recruiting students from the Oakland Public Schools and the Allen Temple Baptist Church, and it stresses the importance of conscious thought about content and emphasis in messages to parents and students and the intentional development of a relationship with the student and caregivers beginning with the very first conversation.

Chapter 5 discusses how we recruited and selected staff for our program and how this process evolved to assure the selection of individuals who would consistently have positive effects on our students' engagement and achievement. PI grappled with possible selection criteria for effective teaching staff, such as schools attended by applicants, GPAs, highest degree attained, scores on various tests, and intuitive beliefs about who would be an effective staff person. Additional considerations surfaced related to the content and scope of the training necessary to prepare teachers to be effective in urban settings. These included the length of staff training, topics covered, who would deliver the training, and how its effectiveness could be measured. We learned from our experiences at Project Interface that many variables that were commonly thought to be highly important often turned out to be less important. In addition to lessons learned through the development of our staff selection process, this chapter provides details of our 2-week staff training session. Related materials used by PI staff are included in Appendix D.

Chapter 6 discusses how we used state standards as a basis for our curriculum content and how we meshed our work at Project Interface with work assigned by the students' schools. Today there are many sources of prepared materials designed especially for the after-school setting. Some of the materials focus on academics, others on youth development and leadership; still others address both. When our program began, the source of the material was a challenge for PI. We received words of caution from colleagues at the University of California at Berkeley to aim high and avoid using dittos or drill-and-kill content with our students. In 1983, the California State Board of Education articulated its standards of achievement for classes and course content; these standards served as the basis for the curriculum content that we created at Project Interface. Chapter 6 also shows how we created learning experiences that were relevant and engaging, while addressing three student needs: filling in gaps of materials that had not been taught and/or learned, assuring mastery of their current work, and introducing them to material they would encounter when they left their math classes and entered college preparatory classes. Appendix E presents a guide to quality standards in curriculum design and development (Figure E.1).

Chapter 7 opens the third section—on direct programming experiences—through presentation of the rules and structure for the study group setting.

PI's approach to rules and routines included firm rules, an explicit effort requirement from students, and frequent parent involvement within a framework of nurture and challenge to help students reach their potential. In the process of creating the rules, we had to decide what rules were fair rules, when to involve parents, and how to get parental support when needed. After-school programs use a variety of approaches to discipline that are based in part on the desired environment and program goals; some strive to create an atmosphere where staff are more like peers than authority figures, and others see themselves primarily as a respite for children. As in many organizations, the philosophies of discipline held by members of the PI community varied; some staff felt comfortable assuming a role of authority and others did not. All staff needed training to be comfortable and effective when involving parents or family members in PI's disciplinary procedure for students. Our board was most concerned with having a standard process for discipline, and the teaching staff focused on classroom management. We had some instances where a parent didn't believe us or the child came back and did the same thing the very next day. However, we were rarely without the endorsement and support of our parents and family members. Appendix F presents PI rules (Figure F.1) and a chart of suggestions for addressing typical student characteristics and behaviors (Figure F.2).

Chapter 8 shares our realization that pedagogy and sensitive instruction were not only a means of engaging students, but also the most important means of nurturing our students so that they could become confident students and high achievers. Most of our students were well acquainted with failure, and though very confident and sure of themselves in many other spheres of their lives, they were not confident in math and science classes. The challenge at Project Interface was not only to engage the students but also to create an environment that would encourage them to try again after having experienced failure in the past. The program used many activities and processes to reinforce the learning process, and over a period of time we identified three important elements that seemed to impact student engagement and, eventually, their achievement: the nurturing program environment, study group instruction, and significant relationships developed between students and study group leaders (SGLs). This chapter provides details on elements of our program structure that were designed to nurture students. Appendix G shows ways that we used Bloom's Taxonomy to guide the development of strategies to encourage and retain student interest (see Figure G.1).

Chapter 9 describes how we perceived our relationships with parents, how they were engaged with the program, and how we established and maintained those relationships. We learned early on that we simply would not be able to retain many of our students long enough to see them grow if we did not have the endorsement and engagement of our parents and caregivers. Students might enter the program excited and ready for anything, but soon the hard realities of work, frustration, and effort would make many of them want to quit and run. Our parents would not let them quit. They supported us in pushing and encouraging our students to achieve their goals. Our perspective on the development of relationships with caregivers is detailed in Appendix H, Figure H.1.

The final chapter of the book is a troubleshooting guide. The process of establishing, maintaining, and growing a new program is fraught with many predictable challenges, ranging from funding, staffing, and recruiting to internal politics. This chapter provides an outline of several of the issues that PI faced as the program experienced growth and development and suggestions for how to handle some common challenges.

After reading this book, there will be many who will say, "That's all well and good for the 1980s, but it's a new day—kids have changed, and they just aren't the same." My response is that it is not the children who have changed as much as it is the adults who decry their behavior and attitudes—and frequently with justification.

My own experiences with "today's youth" give me much cause for hope. I worked with a group of middle school girls in Washington, D.C., in 2003. They were unruly; rude; ill-mannered; disrespectful; belligerent; concerned about boys, hair, nails, and lip gloss—and they refused to work. I asked whether parents had been called, and I was told that parents did not care, would not come, or could not be reached. I wanted to learn whether or not I could contact the parents, establish a positive relationship, and get changes in behavior from the girls, one of whom announced to me, "We women in here," and challenged, "Who are you?" the day that I met them. I wound up driving to public housing complexes as well as calling parents at work and on weekends. Taking the advice of a friend, I called and asked the father of one student to ask his child to call me. She did. I asked her whether we could work this out ourselves or if we needed to involve her father. Without hesitation, she said, "We can work it out." I stated the terms and conditions that would keep the conversation between the two of us, and she stated, "Alright." With the exception of one parent, all of them responded positively, and I saw immediate behavior changes. Establishing mutually supportive relationships with parents worked for Project Interface in the 1980s, and it will work now.

Acknowledgments

I AM DEEPLY grateful to many people for their unfailing support, counsel, and encouragement during the writing of this book. The book would not have been written without the initial interest of Etta Hollins, as well as the commitment of Brian Ellerbeck and his staff at Teachers College Press to see the process through to completion. I am especially indebted to Patrice Johnson. Her balanced, objective, yet empathic perspective was invaluable to me. Her experiences and perspective enabled her to go right to the essence of an issue while capturing the nuances and implications involved. Her writing and editing skill oftentimes helped clarify what I was trying to say, and her ability to structure and sequence tasks were instrumental in getting the job done. She acted as a collaborator in the content and presentation of all the Appendixes, perhaps a minor component of some works, but an absolutely critical part of this one. If she had not offered consistent, supportive involvement, I doubt it would have been completed.

I was inspired by the vision, faith, nurture, and high expectations of the Allen Temple Baptist Church and the Northern California Council of Black Engineers.

I would also like to acknowledge my mother, Anne Gainer, and brother, Charles Bouie. I would not have completed this book had it not been for the numerous friends over the years who have shared their experience, strength, and hope with me, and for me, especially Helen Potter. Their fellowship has nurtured and sustained me. Curtis Smothers's persistence in asking, "When is the book coming out?" every time I returned to California held my feet to the fire.

I am forever grateful to the staff at Project Interface. Among the many who were present over the years, Julie Kuo, Angela Logan, Leo Oseguerra, Michael Spight, Program Manager, and Study Group Leaders Rolando Manrique, Stephanie Nichols, Shawuan Anderson, Damone Hale, Timothy Bodine, Allan Krone, Rashael Hollins, Shawn Moss, Omar Yousef, Malik Wajiid, Brandon Mendiloa were among the finest. They did so much with so little, and their willingness to roll up their sleeves and stay the course was a source of endless delight and inspiration. They kept their eyes on the prize: our children and their families.

So many stories of courage, commitment, and effectiveness fade away unappreciated, misinterpreted, or unacknowledged. I am humbled and grateful to be able to share this one.

After-School Success

CHAPTER 1

The Guiding Philosophy and Initial Plans for Project Interface

If you are behind, that means you have to run twice as fast.
—Booker T. Washington, *Up from Slavery*

THIS CHAPTER introduces you to the Elmhurst District, the neighborhood where Project Interface was located in East Oakland, and to the two organizations that collaborated to form Project Interface (PI), an experiment in alternative education for underachieving middle school students. I share the story of the founding of PI as an answer to the need for programs that challenge students to reach their potential academically and provide them with a culturally appropriate learning setting. First, I describe some of the problematic facts and statistics about the Elmhurst District. Then I outline the prevailing theories of the traditional sociological view that used these facts as a basis for ineffective policy and program design. Next, I describe the two organizations that joined to create PI—the Northern California Council of Black Professional Engineers and the Allen Temple Baptist Church—and the common vision and goals of these organizations that led to the new program. In the following section I share the individual visions of key people who were instrumental in the initial stages of the program's development and implementation in their own words; and I share how I came to work at PI.

In the *"Lifting the Program off the Page"* section I present some specific examples of ideas to consider in the initial stages of program design. Related materials appear in Appendix A, which contains checklist tools for partnership creation and program design in Figures A.1 and A.2. Appendix Figure A.3 presents possible activities to support after-school programs in relation to the major program elements addressed in this book. The information is presented in the form of recommended actions that can be taken at national, local, or program levels to support creation of effective after-school programs and support planning and direct service efforts to provide quality academic programs.

WHY CREATE AN AFTER-SCHOOL ENRICHMENT PROGRAM IN EAST OAKLAND?

The Facts About Elmhurst

There is no denying the cold, hard facts about the circumstances of students who live in the Elmhurst District of East Oakland, home to 54,000 people in the 1980s, according to 1980 Alameda County census records. By any standard, the students and families in the Elmhurst District confronted an array of daunting obstacles.

Income levels were low, with more than 50% of families earning under $15,000 per year. Almost a quarter of the population, 21.4%, had incomes of $5,000 or less; 8.9% earned $5,000 to $7,499; 7.7% earned between $7,500 and $9,999; 13.8% earned between $10,000 and $14,999.

The Elmhurst District had the highest infant mortality rate in Alameda County. In addition, Elmhurst's unemployment rates for teenagers and men between the ages of 18 and 25 were the highest in the county and reflected the national average of 34% to 50% of unemployment for Black men. Elmhurst was once a hot spot in the city due to a robust trade in crack cocaine, and this contributed to the community's challenges. Moreover, teenage pregnancies were a significant problem, and officials in the district's middle schools reported as many as five pregnancies as of October at their schools.

Finally, student academic achievement was abysmal. On the Comprehensive Test of Basic Skills (CTBS), Black students scored an average of 20 percentile points below White students in grades 1 and 2. In grades 3 and 6, for the same year, Black 3rd graders scored 71 points below White students in reading and 69 points below their White counterparts in math. Black 6th graders scored 65 points lower in reading and 50 points lower in math. By high school, the dropout rate in Oakland was officially 40% and unofficially at 50% for Black and Hispanic students.

The Traditional View

Amid many theories about the effects of poverty and explanations of statistics, anthropologist Oscar Lewis ushered in a new era of conceptualizing the poor in 1959. His ideas formed the basis for the development of policy and programs to serve the poor for many years to come. Lewis believed that a segment of the population within the lower class in modern society had a pathological culture, a culture of poverty.

Lewis (1961) argued that his study of the poor in Mexico City revealed that "most of them are badly damaged human beings" (p. xxx). Taking seriously the relationship between culture and personality, Lewis emphasized the enduring and intractable nature of what he believed was a pathological subculture. He understood culture as a design for living that is passed from generation to generation and believed that the poor developed designs for living in poverty that they passed on to their children in the socialization process. Lewis believed that by living in a pattern of poverty, the poor effectively closed the door on social mobility.

Policy makers in the 1960s used Lewis's thesis to argue that the poor were "culturally disadvantaged" and needed cultural uplift and self-esteem before they could make proper use of the schooling, jobs, and income that accompanied a good education. One of the most influential and far-reaching arguments of this theory was Daniel P. Moynihan's *The Negro Family: The Case for National Action*, which he authored while serving as assistant secretary of labor (Office of Policy Planning and Research, 1965). Moynihan believed that the causes of problems in the Black community could be traced back to a matriarchy produced by slavery and nurtured under segregation. This matriarchy was the cause of a tangle of pathologies that plagued the Black community. While he conceded that matriarchy itself was not inherently pathological or damaging, he deemed it incompatible with the patriarchal structure of American society.

In 1964, Charles Silberman echoed Moynihan's concerns in *Crisis in Black and White*. He concluded that the disorganization of the family is reflected in the disorganization of Negro life itself, producing an absence of the inner strength and self-discipline needed to have control over one's environment (Silberman, 1964).

In the face of these theories, members of a large urban church and a Black professional society joined forces to create an educational program that would nurture urban students and help them overcome the obstacles in their lives. Building on a tradition of self-help, community uplift, and nurture of children that began in slavery, the church and the engineers acknowledged the problems confronting the children and families of the Elmhurst District. However, their cultural context and core beliefs also gave them the ability to see and concentrate on the potential in Elmhurst; Project Interface was the result of a focus on the promise of the children, their families, and the community.

The Vision of the Church and the Engineers

In the early 1980s, the Elmhurst District of East Oakland was home to many vibrant and community-minded organizations and institutions. In the forefront was Allen Temple Baptist Church (ATBC), first organized in 1919 with a membership of 19 people under the leadership of the Reverend J. L. Allen. By the 1980s, it had grown to more than 2,300; as of the 1990s, the count was more than 4,000 members. The church's exponential growth was rooted in its historical role in the Black community as the strongest cultural agent and as the center of community life, resistant to prejudice and dedicated to the nurture of its members, particularly the children. In the tradition of the first churches founded in Black communities, the pastor of Allen Temple, Dr. J. Alfred Smith, was able to use its independent base to promote and lead campaigns advocating for the needs of its constituents.

ATBC's educational portfolio included a tutorial program and an annual fund-raiser attracting 2,000 people and raising $52,000 (Bennett, 1983). In 1982 the church awarded 54 scholarships to college students. An adult education program, Spanish Study, was offered, and released time education (video-taped instruction used subsequently for classes at other times or locations) was held at the church for course credits at Merritt College in Oakland. The church's history of active involvement in education, reflecting the needs of the community, made it a perfect site to house Project Interface.

Allen Temple's partner in the genesis of Project Interface was the Northern California Council of Black Professional Engineers (NCCBPE), one of many professional and cultural societies spawned by the Black church. The antecedents of these societies were the self-help, social, and, later, professional organizations formed by African Americans early in the 19th century, which initially helped runaway slaves escape to freedom and later helped members make progress in society and serve their communities.

According to its members, NCCBPE emerged from an informal gathering of 34 Black engineers throughout the San Francisco Bay area to establish camaraderie and act as a pressure group to enhance the professional and career opportunities of its members. Through many community outreach programs, NCCBPE members tutored college students, organized an annual science fair, provided speakers for college fairs, and coached newly hired engineers as they began their professional careers. ATBC and NCCBPE's shared values and understanding of their community led them to develop a successful partnership to serve their members.

THE VISION OF POTENTIAL AND PROMISE THAT GUIDED US AS WE BUILT OUR PROGRAM

This section includes perspectives of PI's founders in their own words.

Dr. J. Alfred Smith Sr., Pastor, Allen Temple Baptist Church

In 1981, a colleague I worked with at Bishop College called me and told me about funds that were available for minority institutions in math and science education through the U.S. Department of Education's Minority Institutions Science Improvement Program (MISIP). She encouraged me to consider applying for a grant. Allen Temple had already established a scholarship fund and a tutoring program, and my wife taught adult education classes at our church.

I was very excited about the possibility of being awarded a grant in math and the sciences. I knew that we needed such a program because the children attending the neighborhood school across the street from Allen Temple were performing 3 years below grade level. I also realized that, because they were so far behind, upon reaching high school, many of them were not prepared to be members of the college prep track, and those who were able to make it into that track did not have the background that would permit them to study for a profession that required mathematics and science.

It was my vision and hope that Project Interface would address these issues and produce positive results for our children. I asked members of my congregation to work on the proposal. Dr. Vera Ray, an educator in the Oakland Public Schools, wrote the bulk of the proposal. Because of the separation of church and state at that time, Allen Temple could not receive the funding directly. That meant we needed a partner. I remembered that one of the members of the church's deacon board was also a member of the engineering society that often had meetings at our site. I contacted Ben Darden and asked him to serve as the liaison between the engineers and the church. As a result, another partnership was created.

The members of NCCBPE worked with Dr. Ray to define the kinds of activities that would be included in the program and agreed to serve as the project's fiscal agent if it received funding. Allen Temple would provide a physical and spiritual home for the new program. Not only was there trust between the church and NCCBPE; there was also a shared concern about the future of our children.

Eventually, the MISIP grant was awarded to Allen Temple and the NCCBPE. I must say that we achieved success largely because of the leadership of Stanford University–trained Dr. Anne Bouie. She was a lively, enthusiastic motivator. Her knowledge of public education had been honed at Stanford, yet she was not an intellectual snob or an elitist. Her warm and outgoing personality attracted parents and students, and it gave the Allen Temple membership a deep confidence that the project was in good hands.

The project proved to be successful, not only in the challenge of helping those who had a severe academic deficiency in math and science, but also in providing enrichment for students who were gifted and not being challenged by their classes in school. This project, however, could have failed had it not been for the visionary services of Dr. Bouie, who could have placed financial remuneration far above community service.

Anthony Pegram, Member of NCCBPE

I joined NCCBPE in the late 1970s because I needed the support of other Black engineers and I liked what the organization did in the community. Internally, I received coaching and advice from senior engineers, and we developed strategies for coping, advancing, and extending our own individual careers. This was balanced by a lot of community service.

As I became a more active member, I had many rewarding experiences that made me feel that I was giving back to my community and that at least some students were being prepared for high school and college. NCCBPE worked with the director of the East Oakland Youth Development Center (EOYDC) to run SAT preparation workshops for high school kids. EOYDC recruited the students, and we used their facility. NCCBPE members also went to various junior and senior high schools to speak and do workshops, and we organized career fairs and college tours for students. I worked with students from December to April, and I was gratified to see many of them do well and gain admittance to good schools. Even today, a student will come up to me and thank me for what I did.

The proposal to work with Allen Temple on Project Interface actually came at a good time for us to extend our work into the high schools. The NCCBPE charter members were much more activists than the members who were joining by the 1980s, and we were beginning to accept the fact that many members simply were not going to volunteer their time as much as we needed them to. They had needed to fight to get into and stay in school, and it got harder to remind folks that Black engineers are still an endangered species. We began exploring getting paid staff to support our work, so Project Interface meshed with our goals and intentions perfectly. We had worked with the Black engineering students at UC Berkeley, and that's where we got the idea of having college students work with the younger kids; we thought they could bridge the gap and help the children relate to math. In selecting a program director, we wanted someone who had strong community ties and was able to work with kids. Our ideas about what we wanted were pretty similar to the church's ideas, and when we made our recommendation to the church, once again, there was agreement. NCCBPE members were involved there as well; we helped tutor and mentor the college students that the program hired. It was great to see three generations there sometimes: charter members of NCCBPE, the college students, and the junior high school students. That's what it was all about, getting to the children as early as we could and trying to work with them for as many years as we could.

Ben Darden, Member of NCCBPE and the ATBC Deacon Board

I first learned of Project Interface when Pastor Smith apprised me of the possibility of funding for an after-school enrichment program for young people and told me that the church would need a functioning 501(c)3 to administer the grant if it were awarded. I told him that I would take it to the president, Tolbert Young, and that he would present it to the membership of NCCBPE. At our meeting, we considered the costs, liabilities, and level of involvement we wanted—and the level of involvement we could achieve in the day-to-day operation of the program. We really liked the idea because it meshed with our organization's mission and ongoing community outreach work. We were already tutoring college students, we hosted a college night each year, and several of our members mentored students, so there really wasn't too much of a decision to make—it was more about who was going to do what and figuring out the technical details.

Once NCCBPE agreed to become partners with Allen Temple, Pastor Smith appointed Vera Ray and me as church liaisons. NCCBPE's vision of the program was the MESA (Mathematics, Engineering and Science Achievement) model; we wanted a feeder program that started at the junior high school level and worked with children all the way through high school and even into college: that was the vision—to work with them through graduation (Utah State Office of Education, 2006).

When we were interviewing candidates for the position of executive director, we were very concerned with how the director would relate to the kids. We wanted to make sure the person could understand them—as well as anybody can understand junior high school kids—and be able to work with them. The person had to be able to motivate the kids to get the work done. Our other concern was parental involvement—we wanted the parents involved from the very beginning. In addition to sending their kids to the program, they were required to come to meetings themselves. The program wouldn't work without them, so we really were concerned about these two issues.

Anne Bouie, Founding Director

I first learned about Project Interface in 1982, when the senior pastor of the church, Dr. J. Alfred Smith Sr., made a formal announcement about a new program that would serve young people from the community as well as church members. As a relatively new member of the church, I had stopped being surprised by these frequent announcements. Almost every week brought an announcement of a grant, award, or acknowledgment to the church, the pastor, or a member of the congregation. The church is known internationally for its pioneering work in urban ministry, community outreach, and collaborative efforts with a wide array of community groups. While I was always gratified to hear the announcements, this one caught my complete attention.

The pastor announced that ATBC and the NCCBPE had been successful in seeking funding from the U.S. Department of Education's Minority

Science Improvement Program and that the church would house yet another collaborative project, an after-school math and science program for junior high school students. These students were to be tutored and mentored by the program's second target group, math and science majors enrolled in one of the Peralta Community College system's five campuses. The purpose of Project Interface was to create a learning environment for urban middle school students that would motivate them to perform at exemplary levels in school and on standardized tests and through which they would acquire the ability to enter and succeed in advanced math and science classes in high school and in college.

This mission was compelling to me because I was at a critical juncture in my life. I had recently moved to Oakland from Palo Alto, joined Allen Temple, and just finished work on my fourth federally funded technical assistance project. I had had time to reflect on and synthesize what I learned from the technical assistance projects, each of which focused on a specific problem experienced by urban school systems. The first project focused on enhancing the problem-solving capacity of urban schools; the second on the desegregation and integration of schools and classrooms; the third on reducing the percentage of disproportionate suspensions among students of color; and the fourth on reducing violence and vandalism in urban schools. During the projects I learned that the recommendations for policy and practice were quite consistent across content areas. I saw research on best practices confirmed by effective practitioners, who did much of what was suggested by the findings, even when they were not familiar with the research. Most importantly, I observed that effective practitioners all addressed certain issues in similar ways.

The educators I met throughout the projects were young and old, male and female, liberal and conservative, of every ethnic and cultural group imaginable, and from various regions of the country. They were all saying the same things about what they believed and how they worked effectively:

- They had high expectations for themselves, their staff, students, and families.
- They created clear structures and routines that supported staff and students.
- They were conscious of the prevailing theories about poverty and low student achievement but did not subscribe to them.
- They had a clear sense of their objectives.

The educators knew how to build mutually supportive working relationships and create learning environments that produced academic success for students and teachers. I was curious to see whether doing what effective practitioners had done would work for me.

The only disappointing aspect of the entire announcement for me was the fact that a start-up director for the program had already been hired and was ready to begin work. I had turned to pursue other opportunities when it was announced that the woman who had been written into the proposal was leaving the area. She and her husband were missionaries, and they had been called to Zaire for service, so the position was now available. My intense excitement about the position was a strong indicator to me that my attraction to this new program had become more than mere interest.

NCCBPE opened the position for interviews, and I was invited to meet with them. My area of certification was history and social studies, not mathematics and science. Initially, they were concerned that I was not a scientist or an engineer, but they were open-minded enough to talk with me. A great deal of the interview focused on how I could design and run a math and science program without being a scientist. The panel of interviewers questioned me intensely about how I would set the program up and what the students would be taught.

I shared my learning experiences with the engineers, and they seemed to accept the possibility that I could apply what I had learned to Project Interface and that my experiences could be combined with their knowledge of curriculum content to create an effective program. For me, it was a wonderful opportunity to synthesize what I had learned and apply it to the flatlands of East Oakland.

LIFTING THE PROGRAM OFF THE PAGE

This section highlights examples from the creation of PI and suggests ways to incorporate ideas and ways of thinking into concrete and effective strategies for the design of a new program.

1. Reflect on role models and their lessons. Mrs. Dolores Frazier was the principal at Highland Elementary School, directly across the street from Allen Temple. She not only encouraged me to stop smoking, but she also coached me on having good shoes for the office and public appearances as well as walking-around shoes for the playground and the halls. She said I had to be able to walk the halls regularly and that I would learn much by watching and talking with children that I could never learn in other ways.

When we walked around Highland's playground, I watched the way she interacted with children, staff, and parents. I observed that she paid attention to how a child's hair was combed and what that could tell her, who was playing with whom, what student gossip was floating around, and what neighborhood issues were being brought onto the campus. She used what she learned to inform her leadership strategy and her conversations with teachers, children, and their parents. She often knew more about children's interests than their teachers did, and she shared her knowledge with teachers to help them integrate children's interests into their work.

2. *Identify, incorporate, and build on the core beliefs of students, their families, and the community to be in harmony with them.* Being housed at ATBC was a benefit for us because the setting provided a familiar context for our work and allowed us to use the expectations embedded in the environment: respecting elders and authority figures, being on good behavior, working hard and believing in ourselves, and attending to responsibilities. However, even when not operating in a church, one can learn what is important to students and families and how to work in a way that resonates meaningfully in *their* frame of reference.

This means being able to:

- Know and understand the issues that are important for adults in the community
- Know how an adult who has the respect and regard of young people conducts himself or herself
- Know the hopes and dreams, fears and concerns, of adults for their children
- Incorporate as much of the home culture into the structure of the program as possible:
  - Have the orientation at a local church or community facility
  - Invite respected community members to back-to-school night, orientation, and other events throughout the year
  - Explicitly talk about the desire to be a part of the community

3. *Be prepared to explain what you believe, and why, in terms that are meaningful to your constituents.* One educator I know says his parents are not as interested in lifelong learners as they are in lifelong *earners*. They believe if their children are earning, they will be learning *automatically*.

Another educator says that she avoids making judgments or assumptions about parental motives or parenting styles until she has established mutually respectful relationships with the parents. She leads with the assumption that parents love their children and desire to work with her. This enables her to communicate with them in a direct manner without preaching or coming across as meddling where she does not belong. In conversations about student achievement with parents, she uses their language to (1) focus on the goal—the children can and should be doing better in school, (2) share what she intends to do, and (3) acknowledge the fact that she needs parental support.

4. Be open to learning how effective practitioners work. The first time I heard Nick Caputi (an Oakland Public Schools principal) in a workshop, I thought he was a dogmatic authoritarian. He spoke as if he gave his faculty marching orders instead of structure. Fortunately, I had the opportunity to listen to him more than once, and I finally heard what he was really saying. When I actually studied the packet of materials he gave his faculty at the beginning of the year, I saw how he had actually asked them to do work that would help them to be effective in their classrooms.

His worksheets for faculty covered areas such as lesson plans and learning experiences for students by the day, week, grading period, and year; objectives and student assignments for each grading period; and discipline and classroom management procedures to be written, distributed, and taken home for parents to sign. Nick Caputi asked his faculty to develop strategies to help students master the material, to manage discipline problems, and to assess student learning. When teachers completed the packet, they would be ready for their students and for a positive start to the year.

5. Consider a range of issues in building partnerships and designing the program. See Figures A.1 and A.2 for a checklists of areas to consider.

6. Consider the relationship of choices in program design and to local, state, and federal policies that may relate to your program. Appendix Figure A.3 gives an idea of how choices in the development of program components may affect or be affected by local, state, or national policies and trends. It presents ideas and suggested actions relating to each major section of *After-School Success: Academic Enrichment Strategies with Urban Youth* (program goals and partnerships, program preparations, and direct work with children and families) through federal-, state-, local-, and program-level recommendations.

CHAPTER 2

Moving Through the Bowels of Bureaucracies and Organizations to Gain Access to Your Students

You'd be amazed at how much you can get done if you don't care who gets the credit.

—Curtis Smothers, personal communication

BUILDING relationships with the adults in systems and organizations is the first step toward finding students with whom to work directly. Goodwill and strong relationships with adults are the context needed to create an environment where students feel safe and accept the fact that their best is expected of them. As we will see in later chapters, sometimes relationships with the adults are more essential than those with the children. Often, the children will not allow you to help them if there are no relationships with the adults that they love and respect. Doreen Anthony, a board member, said:

> I think people feel more comfortable sending their children to Project Interface, even if they are not members of Allen Temple. The church is a place that is familiar and feels comfortable. The kids see their parents acting comfortable and agreeing with the staff people, so they know from the very beginning that the parents support the program.

A successful strategy for recruitment will be approached as an opportunity to develop a solid partnership with the adults who will play an ongoing role in support for your program. If recruitment is approached as a task to be done that requires interaction with people in various organizations, it will not serve the program, staff, or students in the long run, because students' achievement goals and expectations are rooted in the organizations in their communities and the experiences of the adults in their lives.

In this chapter I share my experiences of gaining access to students with two major organizations that were critically important to PI, the Oakland

Public Schools (OPS) and Allen Temple. The "School Systems" and "Churches or Community Organizations" sections include descriptions followed by portions on message framing and initial meetings that show the development of our communication framework and relationships in each system. After identifying the individuals who will be involved in the development of the program, you will need to take time to frame and shape your message for each meeting so that it addresses the perspectives and concerns of different individuals. You will have the opportunity to make allies and garner support from each person with whom you talk. Even if you do not make an ally, you get a sense of where your opposition lies and what you can do about it. In the "Turning Bureaucracies into Partnerships" section, I share some ideas on how to integrate key points into a strategy.

SCHOOL SYSTEMS

Levels of Hierarchy in School Systems

Urban schools are approached by many different organizations, each with its own agenda. As a result, school systems are often weary and jaded when yet another enthusiastic and caring person believes that his or her program is the missing solution. A willingness to invest time to learn about schools and organizational systems and an ability to clearly describe your goals will be crucial to your success in developing relationships with the adults with whom you will work. The first concern in working with large bureaucracies is identification of the offices and individuals with whom you need to talk.

Typically, teachers and counselors will not work with you unless you have approval from their principal. The principal will not allow you to work on his or her site without the knowledge and approval of the appropriate administrator at the central office. Frequently, this individual will need the direct approval of the superintendent and, in some cases, the board of education.

In some systems, the central office administrator of contact may be an area superintendent or cluster leader, who has jurisdiction over a set of schools within the district, and may have the authority to grant you access to his or her domain and assume responsibility for informing the superintendent and board of education him- or herself. However, the central office may require you to gain approval from the board of education, which, in turn, will not place you on its agenda until you have central office approval.

To gain access to school sites, you will need to learn which office is responsible for after-school programs. You can try the associate superintendent or the director of special programs. Initially, it may be the superintendent him- or herself. If you do not know where to start, call the superintendent's office or the office of public relations and ask to be directed to the appropriate office. Once you have a thorough understanding of the layout of a school system and the approval process, you will be ready to develop relationships with the people inside the school system.

School Systems Run on Relationships, Not Organizational Charts

From the outset, relationships were involved in implementing PI. Dr. Vera Ray, an OPS administrator and co-author of the proposal, steered me to the correct central office administrator, the associate superintendent for instruction, Dr. David Swanson. Dr. Ray had already vouched for the program by sharing her involvement with Dr. Swanson. Even though Dr. Swanson would not be directly involved with PI, he wanted to know what we intended to do and where we wished to work.

If PI had not had the advocacy of Dr. Ray, we might have taken a different approach by talking with a site administrator, to ascertain interest in working with us, and taken this information with us when talking with Dr. Swanson. As long as I make clear to the principal that I intend to meet with the area or associate superintendent and want to share the fact that site administrators are interested in working with me, the chain of command has been respected. I remember meeting with one principal who said:

> Thank you for coming to talk with me, even though you gained access to the school from Dr. Swanson. I do not appreciate it when somebody just walks into my school and tells me what they intend to do just because they met with the superintendent or know somebody else downtown. I am the one who's going to be held responsible if something goes wrong, and I do have the prerogative to say no to a program. Walking into my school without talking with me and asking to become involved here is like walking into my house without ringing the doorbell.

Clearly, I had to establish a working relationship with the principal in order to have access to teachers and students. Even though I had permission to work with the school through central office approval, that access was tenuous until I had received the genuine endorsement of the principal. Successful relationships with people who will support your program will depend in part on your ability to frame your messages to them and to their communities effectively.

Framing Your Message: Where They Stand Determines What You Say

This is the way I framed the work we intended to do at Project Interface for the school district. First, I put myself in the position of central office and site administrators, counselors and teachers, and developed answers to these questions:

- How does the work complement any existing programs in the district as a whole and/or the schools where I want to work?
- How does our work directly address the district's mission statement, strategic plan, and/or stated annual goals and objectives?
- How does our program directly address improving student academic achievement, engagement with learning, and/or performance on standardized tests?
- What do I need from the district and/or school sites to do my work? How often do I need it, and from whom?
- How disruptive to the site's routine will the work be? Do I need shared space on the site? Does the project need access to school equipment or supplies?
- Who requires a report or update on the work, and how often?

It is also helpful to prepare answers to the questions in advance and to create a fact sheet or a program brochure.

In addition to abbreviated answers to these questions, your project fact sheet can also share this kind of information:

- Your project mission
- The program location and contact people
- The population whom will you serve
- The program components or activities
- A schedule of direct services delivered by the program
- Your staff list
- Your board member list

Project Interface designed a general program brochure to show what we did, fact sheets to use when recruiting volunteers from professional organizations and corporations, and a volunteer interest form to collect information from parents and other potential volunteers. The Project Interface brochure can be viewed at www.annebouiephd.com.

Initial Meetings and the Role of School Staff in Recruitment

When we were first making contacts with principals, one stated, "Well, you know, at this level, I really don't have much contact with students; you will have to talk with my counselors"—and we were happy to do so. Another said, "This could help us; I know several students that could be doing better and are not! Make sure the counselor includes them on the list he makes up for you!"

Our first contact with one of our principals was early one morning when we found him in front of the school talking with his students and herding them into the building. He was in the middle of a sea of children. I could see that he was enjoying himself and that students were paying attention to what he said to them. He told us:

> Having high expectations for the students is the key. You have to keep them up, and not only let them know that you believe in them, but that you actually expect them to do the hard work. Being out here first thing in the morning lets me do my little informal pep talks and start the day on point: It's all about the learning.

Whether principals were detached or hands-on administrators did not matter as long as we were successful in communicating with them. When we met with principals, we were careful to describe the particular segment of the student body we wished to work with, why we wanted to work with them, and what the school could expect as a result of our work. Unlike many programs, we did not need space or meeting time with the faculty or staff. We shared our goals, invited them to our site, and at each school we were referred to the appropriate counselor who helped us identify potential students and set up our first meeting with them at the school.

When PI began, middle schools in Oakland had three counselors, one for each grade level. Given their responsibility for as many as 300 students, we worried that counselors would overlook the bright, underachieving kid acting up in the corner who was really smart, in spite of the fact that he was flunking general math. We need not have worried. There were so many students enrolled in general math that one program could not have served them all. We were pleased at how well counselors knew their students and understood the kind of student we were recruiting. Our first meeting with a school site counselor went well. The counselor said, "Oh, yes, we have quite a few students who could do better with a little attention or one-on-one help." Another said, "Oh, I'm just who you're looking for," and rattled off several names and promised that she "absolutely would make sure they were at our first meeting with students."

In addition to identifying students, counselors sent announcements to teachers about letting students attend our recruitment meeting and provided passes for them to return to class. The counselors were the final step in the process before we met the students themselves.

Development of mutually supportive relationships with the people you meet in organizations is beneficial in the short and the long term. Several years into Project Interface, a principal we had worked with, Barbara Daniels, was promoted to the central office. She became the district lead in a new multiyear project funded by The Edna McConnell Clark Foundation. She suggested Project Interface as the community partner for this districtwide project. This resulted in additional funding and an increased number of schools and students for our program. In another instance, we learned of a state-funded program from Paul Brekke-Meister, a staff member on loan to OPS from a local county supervisor's office. We submitted a proposal to the state office of juvenile justice and received funding for several years. While making presentations to reviewers at this funding source, we attracted the attention of the program officer at a major foundation, who eventually funded the position of development officer for Project Interface.

CHURCHES OR COMMUNITY ORGANIZATIONS

Systems for Education-Related Activities in Black Churches

My experience as a church member in other Black churches helped me know how important it was to learn the structure of Allen Temple. Most churches in the African American community, regardless of denomination or size, formally address education in one way or another. Most have several of the following:

- Scholarship programs whereby members contribute to send the church's children to college
- An Education Day program at which a guest speaker will talk and all the church's students will be recognized at the beginning of the year
- A graduation or year-end program at which all the church's graduates, from the youngest to the oldest and at all levels of education, are acknowledged
- A roster with the names of all the young people away at college printed in the church bulletin so that members of the congregation can communicate with them
- A formal acknowledgment by the pastor at each report card period

- A formal education department, committee, or board, headed by a church member with significant responsibility and authority for programs, outreach, and activities at the church.

Before your initial appointment at a church, do a little homework by calling the church office to learn as much as you can about the church's educational program and the appropriate person to contact. In addition, it does not hurt to attend a church service before making an appointment.

Most churches have a place in the formal program where visitors are acknowledged. Some churches ask people to "say a few words." This is an opportunity to introduce yourself and begin to convey your understanding of what education has traditionally meant to the church.

Even if you are not asked to speak, your presence is an important way to show your desire to learn about and work with the church. After most services, there is a fellowship hour, where coffee and refreshments are shared. This is another opportunity to meet and greet, because people will approach you with a welcome and an invitation to return. This is a perfect time to request a meeting with the chair of the board of Christian education or its counterpart in the mosque, temple, synagogue, or other organization that you visit.

This small investment in time pays huge dividends because you develop relationships with the adults who are significant in the lives of children.

Framing Your Message for Initial Meetings at the Church

The initial introductory meeting with the pastor, church staff, or lay volunteers has to accomplish several things. First, learn as much as possible about what the church is already doing, and what it wants to do in the future, regarding its youth. Most churches already have youth programs and are always looking for support and reinforcement of these programs. Second, share and explain exactly what your program does—its goals, mission, and the results you seek when working with children. This is another opportunity to use the fact sheet and program brochure discussed in detail earlier in the "Framing Your Message: Where They Stand Determines What You Say" section. Third, communicate a desire for a working relationship with the church, even if it is no more than visiting on Education Sunday. Fourth, request an opportunity to speak with the congregation and share your program. Further opportunities to be involved at the church will only occur if a successful relationship is established at the initial meeting and maintained afterward with the individuals or committee members present.

Your presentation strategy for the congregation is different from that for the small-group meeting that precedes it. If you are not a member at a church, it is still possible to create relationships and obtain the endorsement of the church. In order to do this, you will need to acknowledge the past and current efforts of the organization with which you wish to establish a relationship. I did this by acknowledging the traditional role of the Black church and its historical position on education. Anytime I spoke at a church, I began by including a few of these points in my introductory remarks because they placed my work in a framework that resonated with the congregation:

- The church is the primary cultural institution in the Black community.
- The first efforts of Black Americans to obtain an education grew from informal learning sessions held in arbor churches, located deep in the woods away from plantations during slavery, and often resulted in dire consequences for both teachers and students.
- The emerging Black church was the crucible from which all other African American organizations sprang during the pre- and post-bellum eras.
- Sunday school training programs, vacation Bible schools, and children's programs at churches furthered literacy and schooling for Black children.
- There is a long tradition of out-of-school educational enrichment and a high value placed on education by the church community.

I also communicated awareness of current church member efforts to honor this tradition. With modifications, these points may also be included when making presentations to professional societies, civic groups, and cultural organizations.

After you share your acknowledgment of cultural traditions, acknowledge the present work of the church. Let the congregation know of your awareness of their particular church's support of education, current activities, and contributions to the surrounding community. One way in which you communicate respect to the congregation, civic group, or professional society is to do the research required to gain a full understanding of its educational efforts.

Next, share your program goals and components. This is when I stated high expectations for student behavior and effort, conveying awareness that parents and other adults have raised children who know right from wrong and are expected to behave and achieve. The higher the expectations of children, and the more job and college preparation and respect for their family and church community are discussed, the more amens will be heard. Share the program's requirements, hours, guidelines, and how the adults are to be involved. Finally, close with acknowledgments to the pastor and everyone else who attended the initial meeting and an announcement that you will be available to register students and answer questions during the fellowship hour.

In addition to the brochure and fact sheet, you will need an information packet that describes your program in detail and includes an application, schedule, contact information, and other documents that could help a family decide if your program is right for them (see Appendix Figures B.1 and B.2 for examples of the student and parent contracts included in PI information packets). This packet can be given out after a worship service or at the end of a community meeting. Your conversations after a service or meeting will be your first opportunity for direct recruitment with the adults in children's lives or the children themselves.

Once the relationship with the church is established, it requires maintenance. Some ways to do this include the following:

- Send the church progress reports on how its children are progressing in the program. Time the report to be added to the scheduled educational progress sharing time with the congregation.
- Attend the church's Education Sunday program.
- Send announcements about program events and activities to the church and ask that they be put in the church's bulletin. Be sure to include an invitation to anyone in the church to attend. If their children are involved, most churches will be glad to include the announcement.

Activities like these help to maintain the relationship and support the program at the same time.

TURNING BUREAUCRACIES INTO PARTNERSHIPS

This section offers tips based on our experiences in a brief outline of steps taken to develop partnerships and materials in preparation for the student recruitment stage.

1. Learn who the people are whom you need on your team to build a programmatic relationship with schools:

- Visit similar programs and ask about their experiences and for suggestions.
- Attend school board meetings to observe, listen, and identify school personnel who may help you.
- Obtain and review a roster of school site offices and responsibilities.

2. After the principal, the two most important people at any school site are the receptionist and the custodian. Get to know them as well as you know the principal. The school receptionist and custodian know the ins and outs of the school, where everything and everyone are located—or should be. They can make or break your access to students, teachers, and the principal. I made it a point to always introduce myself and spend a moment talking about Project Interface. School secretaries have provided access to the school's copier when I needed "just 10 more sets," provided phone numbers and a quiet place to use the telephone for immediate access to parents, slipped me in to see busy school principals, and seen to it that my calls did not get lost under the proverbial pile of paper. The custodian at Allen Temple, Mr. Lewis, unlocked doors, carried boxes, found materials, moved furniture for us, and frequently stayed with me until the last child was picked up by a family member.

3. Create a brochure and a program fact sheet for use when meeting and talking with school personnel and representatives of other organizations. Examples of our brochure and fact sheet can be viewed at www.annebouiephd.com.

4. Create information packets for students and parents. Bring packets to each meeting you attend. These supporting materials all help to create a picture of your program. Along with the fact sheet and brochure, include for students: a registration card, application materials, a list of ways the program is expected to benefit students, and a sample student contract. For parents, include a permission form, sample parent contracts, and a volunteer interest form. Both packets should include a schedule of your program hours and components, guidelines, and rules. For examples of information we included in information packets, see Appendix Figures B.1 and B.2.

5. Be able to summarize your program's vital statistics: mission, components, client group, location, and track record in a 2-minute elevator speech. As I was walking through the OPS central office building, I happened to pass the research office, and I walked in to learn about it. I chatted with the director, Dr. Joseph Adwere-Boamah, and one of his staff members, Tom Fredette, about Project Interface. By the time the conversation had ended, Dr. Adwere-Boamah had approved an informal arrangement whereby I could receive our students' performance results on the CTBS at the end of each school year.

CHAPTER 3

Community, Contributions, and Credibility

> At Project Interface, when students received recognition they not only
> felt good, they knew they actually had done well.
>
> —PI Board Member

F ROM THE outset, Project Interface was surrounded with community involvement and support. This chapter provides examples of the ways that PI's extended community supported the program. It describes the community sectors that were sources of human and material resources to support PI, and how those sources were involved in creating the board of directors, which was a microcosm of the larger Oakland community. The primary responsibilities of the board were to establish policy and raise funds. The board and community provided monetary and nonmonetary contributions that were important to PI. The chapter also suggests ways that community volunteers can be involved, and it offers strategies to structure their experience so that it is a positive one and leads to greater involvement. The last section discusses program credibility: the extent to which PI did do what it said it would do. Project Interface used two primary sources of data: the experiences of the students, families, and staff who were involved in the program (soft data), and student performance on the Comprehensive Test of Basic Skills (CTBS; hard data), which was obtained from reports produced by the Oakland Public Schools. A summary of PI quantitative data is provided in Appendix Figure C.1. Appendix Figure C.2 is a resource chart that describes desired program elements and can be used to assist planning at a broad level of educational program development.

COMMUNITY SECTORS AND HUMAN
AND MATERIAL RESOURCES

We identified 13 critical sectors in the community that were potential sources for excellent board members, volunteers, and material resources for Project Interface.

22

The Faith Community

Churches that students, staff, and board members attended allowed staff to make presentations and announcements about student involvement and progress. Allen Temple raised an offering on a yearly basis and provided space at no charge to PI.

The Corporate Community

Project Interface received its first grant from Levine-Fricke because an employee shared our work with its president, who later became a member of the PI board of directors. We received science equipment, computers, and laboratory supplies from Xerox and Genentech. KabiVitrum opened its laboratories to our students for hands-on tours; a leading scientist in breast cancer research gave a lecture and demonstration on sickle-cell anemia to our students. Hewlett Packard sent Guest Speakers as role models. Citicorp provided funding for programs and a steady flow of materials. PG&E opened its furniture storage warehouse to us.

The Philanthropic Community

Community, local, and national foundations were major sources of support. We received gifts from $1,000 to $5,000 as well as significant grants from community and national foundations, including the National Science Foundation. Phyllis Waller of the Coro Foundation in San Francisco selected PI as one of the community placement sites for Coro Fellows for several years. The Fellows were bright and creative, became a part of the staff, and made lasting contributions to the program. The title "study group leader" (SGL) was coined by Coro Fellow John Heffernan. Prior to his joining us, we had struggled with an adequate descriptor. Even though our students referred to them as "tutors," we wanted to convey a different message; they were not teachers in the traditional sense of the word, and "group facilitator" was too broad a term for our purpose.

The Educational Community

Project Interface partnered with Oakland Public Schools to win a grant from the Edna McConnell Clark Foundation. OPS also provided access to used textbooks and to CTBS data for our annual reports. An enterprising SGL walked into the summer academy one day with balance beams donated by the Lawrence Hall of Science; another came with beakers, dissection trays, and other materials from California State University at Hayward.

Major Cultural Institutions

Organizations such as museums and libraries can be excellent sources of program support. The Oakland Museum contributed materials as well as training and technical assistance to staff at PI, and it hosted our students for several field trips.

Government at the Local, State, and Federal Levels

Project Interface received government funding from the local, state, and federal levels for various programs.

The Service Sector

Hospitals and fire and police departments can be sources of support. The police officer who served our neighborhood was always welcome on site; a member of the Berkeley Police Department served as a guest speaker.

Professional Societies Organized Around a Particular Area of Expertise

The Northern California Council of Black Professional Engineers (NCCBPE) was instrumental in establishing Project Interface; the organization operated under its nonprofit status for 6 years. NCCBPE was affiliated with NOBECChE (National Organization of Black Chemists and Chemical Engineers). NCCBPE and the Sinkler-Miller society contributed guest speakers at PI and in the Science Enrichment Collaborative.

Civic and Social Organizations and Groups Organized Around a Particular Concern

Civic organizations, such as Friends Making a Difference, the Links, and the Rotary Club (local and national chapters), acknowledge outstanding service and can provide funds, volunteers, and material resources.

Local Branches of National Franchises

A staff member whose second home was the McDonald's at 98th Avenue and East Fourteenth Street asked the manager for coupons for our students. We awarded them at the monthly ceremony to students who had achieved in all four categories.

The Small-Business Community

Many locally owned small businesses will contribute an advertisement in a program fund-raising book or a prize that can be used for students, staff, or volunteers.

Community-Based Businesses and Services

Local mom-and-pop stores can be important partners in the work of a community-based nonprofit. There was a store like this at the corner of 85th Avenue and East Fourteenth Street that our children stopped in every day. Sometimes they would be late because they were purchasing their daily stash of salt, sugar, flour, and grease. One day I walked up the store and asked the owner whether or not he would be willing to make the store off-limits for PI students after 4:00 P.M. When I explained who I was and what we were doing, he was more than happy to do so. Students found a way to get to the store before the daily deadline.

Community-Based Neighborhood Associations and Organizations

Though giving and supportive, the church drew the line when our students wanted to have a dance. However, the East Oakland Youth Development Center (EOYDC) was right up the street and scheduled us with no hesitation.

Additionally, many of the sectors mentioned had organizations serving particular ethnic groups; for example, a professional society of engineers existed in both the African American and Hispanic communities. The same was true for many other civic and social organizations as well as small-business groups.

An organization that identifies as many sectors in as many communities as possible builds a broad base of involvement that has the potential to yield significant human and material resources. Each of these sectors, at each level, is a potential partner and source of board members, volunteers, funds, and in-kind contributions. The path to larger contributions begins with relationships with potential partners.

A Case Study: The Xerox Corporation's Involvement

The Xerox Corporation's involvement with Project Interface began with a field trip to the Oakland office. Lynn Cerda recalls that the corporation was looking to partner with community organizations that had a focus on math and science: "We were on the lookout for community groups to work with, and we heard about Interface from Kevin Anderson."

The field trip to Xerox was one of the first the program organized, and it was also a first for Xerox. The employees were as excited as the students were and had organized an excellent experience for them. Students were organized into small groups and partnered with a Xerox employee. Employees showed how the machines were designed and used, explained different careers, and made the connection to math and science real for our students. Parents accompanied us, and they left excited about the work as well. Students had experienced a partnership among caring adults that focused on their future.

After the field trip, Vatrice Lanier, a member of Bay Area Black Employees Association (BABE), the support group for African American Xerox employees, hosted a meeting where Joseph Samuels, then chief of police in Oakland and a deacon at Allen Temple, spoke and encouraged the group to work with PI.

From there, Xerox involvement snowballed. Vatrice and Lynn became board members, Bronnie Hazelwood served on the development committee, and Kevin Anderson applied for and was awarded the corporation's Community Service Award, which paid his salary while he served a 9-month internship at PI. He focused on development and community involvement, and he took the program to new levels. Xerox led the way in an increase in attendance and number of tables purchased at the Annual Awards Banquet. Bronnie contributed computer skills and upgraded our funding materials, and Lynn Cerda was the most effective leader of the board's development committee during its entire existence. Diane Greene, a senior staff member in Oakland, was invited by Kevin and Vatrice and made a presentation at the Annual Awards Banquet that year.

Kevin's mentor at Xerox was Glegg Watson, a vice president based at the headquarters in Rochester, New York. Kevin asked Glegg to come for a visit to meet with me and members of the board. Glegg came because Kevin asked him to, and later, Bernard Watson, another vice president, came because Glegg and Kevin asked him to come. Bernard sat down with a group of students and later with the SGLs. I remember him coaching them and sharing his strategies. He carried a simple spiral-bound notebook and took notes as students and SGLs were talking with him. One of the SGLs asked him about the notebook. He said:

> This notebook? I carry it everywhere I go. I have a stack of them. I use it in every meeting I attend. I write down the people who were there and even a little diagram as to where everyone was sitting. I

have a record of everything that was important to me that happened in all of the places I go. This helps me plan, remember, and organize my work. It's very simple, it's not flashy, but it works for me. You all will probably be using something like this one day; I suggest you do, because a lot happens, and it happens fast—you need your own record of what's going down.

Bernard was as engaged with the SGLs as they were with him. The gratification he felt showed in his countenance, and he thanked Kevin and me for the time spent with us at PI. Bernard and Glegg would not have even known of our existence if it had not been for Kevin and other Xerox employees. Initially, Bernard and Glegg came to support them, not the project. Kevin opened an important door for PI that allowed us exposure to senior representatives who had powerful influence in the organization. Eventually, these visits resulted in the corporation's contribution of 20 computers and printers to the program. Allen Temple contributed space for The Xerox Computer Laboratory, and students no longer had to make the trek to the College of Alameda for access to computers.

The Xerox example illuminates several characteristics of successful corporate involvement with a program:

- The interests and goals of the corporation and the program meshed.
- The relationship began slowly, with a field trip to the site and a minimal level of involvement by both parties.
- A successful and rewarding first experience led to increased volunteer engagement with PI in a number of areas: development, graphic design, community involvement by the host company, and community involvement by members of a professional organization.
- The increased involvement led to financial commitments and the commitment of a valued employee's expertise at Project Interface.
- This led to:
  1. Increased financial involvement
  2. The involvement of the company's senior staff at Project Interface
  3. A major contribution of equipment: an on-site computer laboratory

The involvement by Xerox employees at all levels occurred over a 3-year time period. This partnership included contributions from Xerox that were rewarding at all levels of the program. Employees participating on PI's board played one of the most significant roles in the partnership.

ORGANIZATION AND STRUCTURE
OF THE BOARD OF DIRECTORS

In an organization, the board sets policy; the staff implements it. The board raises money; the staff is a responsible steward of the money. The board is the primary advocate for the program; the staff run the program effectively and in keeping with the organization's goals and mission.

Since the focus of our program was on math and science, we were especially interested in corporations, businesses, and organizations in these areas, and our board reflected this. Our board also reflected the fact that we were a community-based program housed at a church; a board member who represented Allen Temple served as a liaison to the church.

The individuals representing the various sectors not only brought their professional expertise and their individual strengths and interests to the board; they also served as reference people who were knowledgeable about influential organizations and individuals in their area of expertise who could provide access and credibility to a new program.

Our first chairperson, Howard Smith, was from Silicon Graphics, a leading company in Silicon Valley. Howard brought immediate credibility to our organization in an area that was as important as the endorsement received by being housed at Allen Temple. His presence paved the way for members from the banking community and corporate communities to accept invitations to serve.

There were four standing committees on PI's board of directors:

- The executive committee consisted of all the officers and the executive director. It met on an as-needed basis, monthly or quarterly.
- The fiscal oversight subcommittee was chaired by the board treasurer and made reports to the board on a monthly or quarterly basis. At PI, the accountant submitted the financial reports to the treasurer, who took them to the board. This committee also reviewed and presented the annual budget to the board.
- The personnel subcommittee reviewed all new positions and candidates; it also reviewed recommendations for hiring before they were taken to the board.
- The development and fund-raising subcommittee designed the year's fund-raising activities and organized the development work for the board as a whole.

A different volunteer board member led each committee. Often, committee leaders were trying out a new leadership role or area of focus for the first time.

I did not realize the extent to which board members viewed the experience as an opportunity for personal and professional growth until I interviewed several of them in the process of writing this book. Lynn Cerda, formerly at Xerox, said, "I got a lot more than I gave; I learned so much and had an opportunity to work with a program that not only met my company's concerns, but my own as well." She served as chairperson of the development committee and organized the first telephone drive for our program. She was aware of the need to increase individual donors to supplement other funds.

Doreen Anthony was impressed by the diversity on the board; there were members with so many different professions and different points of view, yet they were "all in accord about the children."

Vatrice Lanier echoed these comments: "Before I served on the board, I was not a confident public speaker, but serving there and working with so many different people helped me grow as a person and as a professional. By the time I left, I had served as president." The personal connection and investment of board members is essential for a strong board.

The chair of the board is a critical position, because the executive director must work very closely with that person on a regular basis; this person sets the tone for the board and its direction. Curtis Smothers assumed leadership as PI was making the transition from a single program to an organization. His ability to form alliances with the likes of Don Duffy, vice president at Kaiser Permanente, helped establish an advisory board whose mission was to implement a capital campaign for permanent space for Project Interface.

EFFECTIVE FUND-RAISING
FOR MONETARY CONTRIBUTIONS

A solid fund-raising document portfolio consists of several documents that can be modified as needed. The annual report is discussed at the end of this section.

The Case Statement

The case statement was a formal document that made the case for the organization. It presented the needs and circumstances the program addressed in the immediate area. It told how we intended to address these circumstances, why the approach was unique, how it connected with existing efforts, and why we choose to do what we did. It stated the program's origins, mission, goals, program components, and outcomes. It placed the work within the context of the field in which we worked. It was usually 10 to 12 pages in length. It was an excellent document for prospective board members, funders, volunteers, or contributors of in-kind gifts.

Letters of Intent

Most foundations and many corporate sponsors requested a letter of intent (LOI) before asking for a full proposal. The letter of intent was an abbreviated case statement (two to five pages in length) that covered the organization's mission, program components, goals, and results to date. It also stated how additional funds would be used, and it presented a brief summary of our short- and long-term goals. Interface had two versions of the LOI. One was three pages long, and the other was five pages. The shorter one was useful for following up with telephone calls to foundations and was always useful for corporations and small businesses. The longer version went into more depth on program components, needs, outcomes, and reasons for the request for funds; it was usually sent when requesting a large amount of funding.

Supporting Documents

These materials supported the case statement and proposals; it also brought the human dimension to formal papers. They included testimonies from clients and current volunteers, samples of work created at the program, and summaries of test result data. We compiled a summary of annual scores on the CTBS test and created a document showing the number of students who transferred to college prep classes in math and science as support materials. We also enclosed samples of science curriculum materials and letters of support from people who knew our work and whose opinions were highly respected in the community.

Standard Documents

These materials were always included in communications with potential funders:

- Roster of the board of directors
- Roster of advisory board members
- Summary biographies of key staff
- Summary of student scores on the CTBS

This information provided brief snapshots of parts of our program. Much of this information was also included in our annual report.

The Annual Report

The annual report was an excellent way to give readers an introduction to the program, and Project Interface devoted the time and energy needed to produce a reader-friendly report. The core of the report presented student performance on the CTBS and transfers to college prep classes. It also provided an opportunity to acknowledge and showcase all of our volunteers, role models and mentors, corporate sponsors, and activities. It was useful to present to prospective board members and was a good supporting document for funding applications.

NONMONETARY CONTRIBUTIONS

Fund-raising at Project Interface was supplemented by an array of nonmonetary contributions from all of the sectors identified earlier. Page 26 of the 1986–1987 PI annual report shows examples of in-kind contributions the program typically received each year from various sources and is available at www.annebouiephd.com. There were four categories we especially desired.

Technical Expertise

Technical experts assisted our program's work and operation. Members of professional societies helped us when our computers went awry. Early on, during a meeting, Pat Marino, foundation manager at the Clorox Corporation, said, "Anne, you need a case statement. Do you have one?" Not only did I not have one; I did not know exactly what she was talking about. She gave me articles on case statements and sample letters of intent; later she reviewed the material once it was written. The board needs technical expertise in all areas; finance, development, and strategic planning are particularly important. Board members should be selected based on the sector they represent as well as their expertise in critical areas.

Role Models for Staff and Students

Twice a month role models came to Project Interface. They provided powerful support for the program. Many role models were scientists and engineers, and others came from a variety of professional fields. We asked guests to talk about their education and career paths and to share personal experiences with difficult situations in their lives.

Guests were able to engage our students and provide them with a variety of perspectives and outlooks on life. They enhanced the experiences of students in the program by expanding our learning community. One guest, Sergeant Reginald Lyles of the Berkeley Police Department, did more than simply come and talk. He brought a display case exhibiting illegal substances, talked about each of them, shared experiences with having to arrest people under the influence of drugs and alcohol, and described what those people experienced in jail or prison. Students sat in rapt attention, asking one question after other. Sergeant Lyles accomplished more prevention in that one day than we had all year long. The impact on students is described fully through several detailed examples in the "Guest Speakers as Role Models and Mentors" section of Chapter 8.

In-Kind Contributions

In-kind contributions saved Project Interface a great deal of money. The program received everything from furniture to binders, computers, rent, science equipment, and office space at school sites. In-kind contributions were often the first phase of a long-term relationship that might eventually include actual financial support. These contributions were publicity opportunities for the program and the donor, and they helped increase the audience that knew about our work.

Career Exploration and Field Trip Sites

All of the scientific companies that Project Interface partnered with hosted career exploration visits for students in which practicing scientists conducted experiments, distributed goggles and lab coats, and walked our students through laboratories. One scientist was working on a cure for sickle-cell anemia at KabiVitrum; a student sat transfixed and said, "My sister has that." A photographer from the *Oakland Tribune* accompanied us, and photographs from the trip were in the newspaper. Companies enjoyed the public relations opportunities, and our students were provided with real-world applications of math and science.

CREDIBILITY

A program's credibility rests on whether or not it does the things it says it will do. Project Interface was a results-driven program that declared it could raise student academic engagement, effort, and achievement. The way we defined success and program effectiveness was important for organizational sustainability as well as for program implementation. Our program had to meet our goals, and the board had to be able to explain how the program worked in order to raise money.

When I started work at Project Interface, I called and asked a former colleague for his thoughts on setting up an evaluation design for the project. I was shocked and disappointed when he suggested that I stay away from standardized test data, help them finish their homework, and focus on variables such as how the students felt about the program. I had worked with this individual in the past and was stunned to realize that he did not believe the students could achieve to the extent that their scores would be worth reporting. This made me even more determined to create a positive effect on student outcomes.

A great deal of pride and self-confidence was generated by the organization's success in meeting its goals year after year. Students entered not carrying books, not doing homework, getting Cs and Ds in general math classes or failing pre-algebra math classes and being transferred back to general math classes. They entered with "attitudes," almost daring us to teach them, rolling their eyes while their parents wrung their hands.

People wondered what the "magic" was that transformed apparently unengaged students, who put forth more effort on nail polish than their homework, into students who got As and Bs, and transferred into and did well in algebra and geometry classes.

Our quantitative results became the core of our fund-raising efforts. I told our staff:

> We compete for money with programs that serve people who are sleeping under *other people's cars*—they don't even have cars of their own. People who fund us appreciate the fact that we love our children and that they have a safe place to go, but they also appreciate results. They desire positive outcomes, and that's a fair ask, because we can do it, and so can our students.

A summary of data for scores on the CTBS during 1982–1989 appears in Appendix Figure C.1.

Presenting the hard data on student achievement was our way of addressing the often felt but rarely expressed belief that urban students of color could not be expected to perform well in school. Many people believed that the best that could be done was to provide a safe place where they could feel good about themselves because their lives were hard and prevented them from doing well. PI's quantitative data showed the success in our program and an alternative viewpoint regarding the potential of urban students.

In addition to the quantitative results—hard data—we also presented soft data: stories about the experiences of students, staff, and volunteers.

Many of these stories appear in Chapter 8. Testimonials brought the numbers to life and allowed participants to share their feelings and experiences in their own voices.

Different groups used the information in different ways. Parents desired proof the program helped their children; funders desired assurance they were making a sound investment; volunteers needed to know they were making a difference. All audiences had to be touched in both heart and mind, because cold facts without the warmth of testimonials did not create the bonding and sense of community needed when the village really does raise the children. However, warm testimonials without evidence that goals were being accomplished would have left children and others feeling shallow, as if all we could produce was a touching story. Both kinds of data were essential for effective programming. See Appendix Figure C.2 for additional detail on characteristics of effective programming.

CHAPTER 4

Recruiting Program Participants

The harvest is plentiful, but the laborers are few.
—Matthew 9:37, King James Version

T HE INITIAL steps of our recruitment process with school personnel, organizational partners, and families of our students were described briefly in Chapter 2. This chapter focuses on our experiences recruiting an even more challenging audience—the students themselves. The students are the essential group to convince because without students there will be no program, regardless of the quality of the facility, the abilities of the staff, or the design of the curriculum.

The chapter describes the core themes of our message to students and how we captured their attention and interest after deciding on our target group. Three themes emerged as the most important points to consider in framing our message for students. The first was the developmental stage of early adolescence. The second was the impact of repeated failure in school over time on their motivation to come to a program 2 to 4 days a week for 2 hours a day; and the third was the need to take away the stigma of failure and create a sense of hope. The chapter also suggests an application process that helped increase student interest and commitment to the program and addresses challenges in the recruitment process. The last section of this chapter, "Engaging Prospective Students," highlights some suggestions to keep in mind when framing a message for students.

RECRUITMENT STRATEGIES

Defining Your Target Audience

Project Interface stumbled on its target population. I encountered the director of an existing program working with math and science students at one of the middle schools with which we hoped to work. I shared the intentions and goals of the program. He shared that his program was already working in several schools, including our target: They were working with students enrolled in algebra and their teachers, and he implied there was no room for another program.

I went back to my office and thought about the implications for Project Interface. We did not want to engage in a turf battle over students and teachers. One look at student performance on the Comprehensive Test of Basic Skills (CTBS) showed that the students already enrolled in algebra were a very small percentage of the student body. Most students were below grade level and enrolled in math classes that did not prepare them for algebra and geometry. The few who were enrolled in college preparatory classes were often struggling. We had already heard reports that students who were enrolled in pre-algebra or algebra and did poorly were not encouraged to get help but were demoted to general math classes. The encounter with the program director resulted in a change of PI's original intention to work with students already enrolled in college prep classes.

The program's mission came into focus more clearly, based on the student population we decided to serve. It was at this point that our "elevator conversation" (a conversation that explains your work in 2 minutes) was created: Project Interface works with middle school students who are underachievers and are not doing as well as they can and should be. Our goal is to begin with 7th and 8th graders and, at the end of 3 years, see to it that they are prepared to enroll and do well in geometry and biology as sophomores.

Getting to Know Your Target Audience

I remember following a counselor at King Estates Junior High School as she led me down the hall to a room full of bright-eyed, curious students waiting to talk with an adult visitor about a program that was completely new to them. They were apprehensive and so was I, even though I had given this meeting as much, if not more, thought than those held with the adults. What could I say to a group of junior high school students that would entice them to come down the hill to Allen Temple 2 hours a day twice weekly, and after the first 2 years of the program, 4 days each week, to study mathematics and science after having been in school all day?

During my preparation for meetings with students, I realized that I was actually more nervous and unsure about talking to them than I was with school personnel and their parents. School personnel immediately understood what I was doing, and principals at each of the home schools where we did most of our recruiting were helpful and supportive. Parents were also responsive and wanted their children enrolled. Once I got past the adults, I learned that the students were the real challenge and that they needed a different message from the one shared with the adults in their lives.

The meetings held at school sites with students identified by counselors consisted of a dialogue with students based around a series of questions like these:

- What is college?
- How many wanted to go to college?
- What did they want to be when they grew up?
- How many knew what mathematics course they needed to enroll in as 10th graders if they wanted to go to college? What science class? How about the 11th and 12th grades?
- How many believed that people did well in school because they were "smart"?
- How many thought they would *really* get to go to college?
- How many would really be willing to do what it would take to get there—assuming they knew what that was?

Developmental Issues in Early Adolescence

One of the more informative documents I came across was a chart listing the characteristics of the typical child during the early and middle adolescent stages. Most of our students were between 12 and 15 years of age, and, as I read the chart, I could not help but smile. The list helped me organize my observations and interactions with students, learn how to best use their developmental growth to help them, and confirmed some of my beliefs about them. The developmental characteristics helped me begin to frame my message to them. For example, middle school students typically do the following (Ozretich & Bowman, 2001):

- Develop new thinking skills, such as thinking more about possibilities, thinking more abstractly, and seeing things as relative instead of absolute.
- Practice new thinking skills through humor and by arguing with parents and other adults.
- Exhibit continued egocentrism and often feel invulnerable.
- Experience changes in their bodies, which can negatively impact their self-image.
- Girls experience pressure to conform to gender stereotypes with the onset of puberty and might show less interest in math and science.
- Minority youth explore many patterns of identity formation, including ethnic identity, bicultural identity. They may also deal with assimilation into or alienation from the majority culture.

- Exhibit extreme forgetfulness, especially between ages 11 and 14.
- Rebuff physical affection and verbal support but still desire and need it. (I learned to ask young men in particular, "Do you still hug?" The response was usually a self-conscious "yes," and an equally self-conscious hug.)
- Exhibit a greater focus on peer friendships, particularly those based on perceived similarities, as they develop an identity outside the family.
- Are confronted with moral and ethical decisions that they are unprepared to handle appropriately.

Because I was conscious of the fact that many of my potential students were unsure of themselves, their future, and where they would be, I could address these issues in my interactions with them.

To help them begin to understand why they needed to prepare for the 10th grade, even though they were only in 7th or 8th grade, I would say:

> You guys are now in the 7th and 8th grade. Just 3 years ago, you were in 4th and 5th grade. Four years ago, you were in 3rd and 4th grade. You know how you really feel about grade school kids—you don't want to be around them, and you don't want them hanging on to you. Yet just a minute ago, you were one of them.
>
> If you fast-forward, in just 3 years, you will be in the 10th and 11th grades; in 4 years, some of you will be graduating from high school, because it happens just that fast. What are you going to be doing? Where do you want to be going?

I could address the self-consciousness around gender roles and expectations by telling the girls, "You have to be cute and intelligent"; I would ask the boys if they "really thought anybody was going to want a man who was not about something?" I addressed the identity issue head-on:

> Have you ever stopped to think about the fact that all the billboards on East Fourteenth Street in your neighborhood advertise nothing except cigarettes, alcohol, cars, and fried chicken? Have you ever thought about the fact that Black people in the newspapers are always athletes, entertainers, or criminals? Well, that is not all there is, and you can be African American and you can still do well in school and go on to college. Where is it written that you can't do both?

Project Interface had to know the issues that accompanied the developmental phases of our students and the social issues they were confronting during this vulnerable period of their lives. The recruiting pitch had to integrate that knowledge using examples, words, and issues that emerged from their experiences and their subjective reality, in order to connect students' future goals with where they were presently in a way that was meaningful to them.

REPEATED FAILURE IN SCHOOL AND PROVIDING HOPE

Project Interface students knew they were enrolled in dead-end classes that did not prepare them for high school or college. I still remember a poignant story shared with me years later by a staff member in the Philadelphia Public Schools because it so powerfully illustrated my experience.

Thelma Miller, an instructional support teacher for King Cluster, Philadelphia Public Schools, was sharing her experiences as a new teacher. Like many new teachers, she was assigned to a class filled with students nobody else wanted. She recollected that, on her first day of class, she enthusiastically said:

> Hello. I'm Mrs. Miller and I'm your teacher. I'm pleased to be here; we are going to have a great year, and we'll be doing a lot of fun things and hard work. I expect you to do well and conduct yourselves as ladies and gentlemen.

As she continued, Thelma said she was interrupted by a voice from the back of the classroom:

> Oh, cut it out, Ms. Miller. We know who we are. We're the dummy class and you're the dummy teacher, so stop that stuff you're talking.

The challenge Ms. Miller faced is identical to the one I faced. How does one get children who have experienced repeated failure in school, year after year, with no apparent relief in sight, to risk trying again?

Repeated failure in school not only resulted in placement in dead-end tracks for students. There were additional consequences; students often had these experiences:

- They had gaps in prior learning that hindered grasping and incorporating new material.
- They had come to believe that intelligence and being "smart" were more important than effort and perseverance in attaining academic success.

- They had experienced success in activities outside of school (at home, in church, or in social and civic institutions) and were self-confident in many areas of their lives, while exhibiting low self-confidence around academic work, accompanied by a belief that they could not do the work.
- They had attended classes with low standards and pedagogy that was not developmentally or culturally appropriate.
- They had not been provided information on careers in math and science; nor were they counseled to enroll in college prep classes or on the relationship between doing well now and going to college.
- They had been bombarded with overt and covert messages that they could not achieve, were not expected to do so, and that it did not matter whether they did or not.
- They had learned coping and defensive skills to mask fear, frustration, and the feelings that accompany experiencing repeated failure at an institution they were required to attend on a daily basis.
- As a result of their experiences, they had developed poor organizational skills and did not effectively organize, prepare, or often complete their work in school.

Empathy and understanding of students' academic experiences and previous opportunities or lack thereof are crucial elements for successfully connecting with, engaging, and retaining students.

I have worked with many individuals over the years who enjoyed school and did well. They had never failed a class, been removed from a college prep class and demoted to a general math class, been sent to the principal's office, or given a detention or suspension. They had not experienced repeated failure or a consistent, yearly assault on their self-confidence and ability to learn. When they were in school, they avoided students like the ones Project Interface served, seeing them as jokers, failures, or uncooperative students. They were frequently unaware of the experiences of their fellow students, even in the very same classrooms with the same teachers. Some, even as adults, were unable to relate to the experience of students who were struggling in school.

My own experiences of failure, ostracism, the dean's office, being made to stand in the hallway, and being sent to the principal's office for cracking my knuckles in class are integrally related to my work. I have been in my students' shoes; I have had firsthand acquaintance with despair, embarrassment, and failure in school, and I know what it took to get me on my feet after I had fallen down. I also know I did not pull myself up by my bootstraps without help, and neither would my students.

Uri Treisman and Robert Fullilove, researchers at UC Berkeley to whom I was introduced by a colleague, provided invaluable counsel that served me well in student recruitment. Uri said:

> Don't call it a tutorial program or a homework program. Don't say the program is about remedial work of any sort. There is a stigma attached to "tutorial" programs, and the students won't come. Tell them it is an enrichment program that will help them prepare for high school and college. Appeal to their pride and the fact that you know they just don't know how to study and organize themselves.

Treisman had had success with the Professional Development Program (PDP) at the University of California, a program he had designed to stop the hemorrhaging of Black students in the gatekeeping chemistry and calculus courses and that had significantly reduce the dropout rates of Black students.

When thinking about what I would share with students, it occurred to me that sharing my own experiences with failure and setbacks might help take away some of the sting that students felt. I told them:

> You know, flunking a class is not the end of the world, and does not mean you are or will be a failure. In fact, the best time to flunk a class is in junior high school, because you sure don't want to be doing it in high school like I was. I had to take algebra two times to get a C, and geometry three times, from the same book and the same teacher, Mr. Peterson, to get a C. Two times for the whole year, and once in summer school, and I still think he passed me because he was tired of looking at me.

Years later, the mother of a former student told me that her daughter had received a scholarship to college, and Leniece said to her:

> When things got rough, I always remembered Dr. Bouie telling us how she had to take geometry three times, so I kept on going.

I saw how important it was to eliminate the stigma of failure and provide students with hope.

The essence of capturing students' attention and earning the endorsement of their parents boiled down to taking their dreams and aspirations seriously; communicating an authentic belief in them, calling on their loyalty to their families and community, presenting them with a reasonable challenge; and providing them with the instrumental means to meet that challenge.

Folk sayings in the African American tradition express these core beliefs:

It's what's inside the balloon that determines how high it will go.

Don't you go [to school, or anywhere else] and make a liar out of me.

Conversely:

Make a liar out of them.

The liar in the second instance was anyone who told students they could not achieve or would not make it in their journey to success.

I quickly learned that students responded positively to the following:

- Stories of other people who had experienced failure on the way to success
- Acknowledgment of their competence in many areas of their lives outside of school
- Affirmation of the fact that they were bright youngsters who needed a challenging enrichment program
- Assurances that there would be help for them, without they or their families being judged
- Admonishments to take the program and themselves seriously, stating and demonstrating from the start the willingness and ability to follow through when necessary
- Appealing to the loyalty to their families, especially their mothers, and their community or neighborhood

After the discussions about students' experiences and desires, PI was presented as an answer to their questions and a way to help them accomplish their goals.

The Student Application Process

After their interest and appetites were whetted, we then shared that Project Interface was a small program and did not have space for all who wanted to attend. Since this was the case, we needed to ask all students who were really interested to submit an essay stating their academic dreams, why they wished to attend Project Interface, and how they felt the program could help them. In addition to the essay, they were required to complete an application, get a caregiver's signature, and return it to the school by a certain date.

The first year, we waited anxiously, wondering whether we would actually get student applications. We did. We received many applications with signatures from parents and caregivers. Students wrote powerful letters about their dreams and ambitions. One wrote:

> I want to come to Project Interface because I want to be somebody when I grow up, I know I need to do good in math and science if I want to go to college. I am not good in these subjects, but I want to do better. I think Project Interface can help me.

Another wrote:

> I think I could do better in school if I had some help. I want to go to college and I want to make my family proud.

And another stated:

> I want to come to Project Interface because it sounds like fun. I can learn more and meet new people.

We were able to take student comments and goals into account in our design of Project Interface.

The Application as an Organizational Tool

A formal application process serves many purposes. First, it requires students to take positive action for themselves. Second, it requires that they act on their interest and assume responsibility not only for completing the application but also for getting it signed by an adult and returning it to the school on time. All these actions go toward building interest and commitment in the student. The work we ask of them at Project Interface has already begun with the application process. Third, the application provides us with a sample of the student's work and competency level without administering a formal test of any sort. Further, we were able to begin planning and organizing based on a fairly accurate count of prospective students.

Finally, we were able to send a formal letter to the students and parents informing them of acceptance to the program and inviting them to attend the student–family orientation. After such a buildup, we had excellent attendance by students and family members and a great deal of anticipation and attention from them as well. It was then up to us to build on and sustain that interest.

Recruitment and Selection Dilemmas

Our recruitment and enrollment process is the one place where we completely deviated from the original proposal that NCCBPE and Allen Temple had submitted. The original proposal states:

> To ensure some degree of success, both junior high school and community college students will be screened. The counselors/advisors of the local junior high schools will be asked to recommend students to participate in Project Interface. Our goal is to identify 150 candidates who will then be interviewed to determine their interest and commitment levels. In addition, the parents will be contacted, and their teachers will be asked to submit recommendations. This screening process will result in the selection of 40–60 participants for the project who will have shown the motivation, parental support, and academic aptitude.

In actuality, we deviated from the target group identified in the proposal for two reasons. First, as the new kid on the block (described in detail in the "Defining Your Target Audience" section early in this chapter), I wanted to avoid a turf battle, especially with the university, which had informed me that it was working in partnership with the algebra classes and their teachers. Second, the overwhelming majority of the students were enrolled in general math classes but had the ability to achieve at a higher level.

We also made changes to the application process. We did not screen or select based on scores and references in the way that the proposal outlined. We did, however, read the student statements to discern student competency levels in writing, and we allowed every student who applied to enter and take the pretest. We knew this; the students didn't.

After we received the students' applications, we read them and telephoned their parents and caregivers, who had already signed the application prior to its submittal and acceptance. We did not take applications without the signature of an adult. The individual signing did not have to be the biological parent, because we knew that students often had numerous adult caregivers and did not always live with a parent. When we received an application with no signature, we would telephone the school counselor and ask for help in getting the caregivers' signature. Usually, students returned with a note or another application page with the caregivers' signature. That was a rule with no exceptions: No caregiver signature, no enrollment.

When we encountered a particularly low-scoring pretest of a 7th-grade student, we were not worried, because we knew that we had an entire year to get the student ready for pre-algebra as an 8th grader. We also enrolled

8th graders who had low scores or who were enrolled in general math. Even though the student would be in pre-algebra, not algebra, as a freshman, we knew we had time to get that student on track as well.

If a student had attended Project Interface and did not enter algebra or pre-algebra as a freshman, we did not ask the student to leave the program. We did not enroll 9th graders who had low scores on our pre-test and who were not already enrolled in algebra because we would not be able to ensure that student's entry into geometry as a sophomore.

The reason for our process was simple: We believed that it was our job to motivate and engage the student and that if we were successful in doing so, the student would begin to demonstrate motivation, engage with school-work, overcome the hurdles of self-doubt, shed the mask of indifference, apply him- or herself, produce the work, and earn the grades and the transfer into college prep math and science classes.

We frequently admitted students who showed little or no enthusiasm for the program. There was one student who was doing very poorly in school and was actually enrolled by her mother. She was very intelligent, defiant, mouthy, and uninterested in anything about Project Interface, except the boys. Her mother gave me the impression that she was washing her hands of the child and turning her over to us. Even so, she was admitted because she was clearly capable and we thought we would have parental reinforcement, which I knew we would need. In this case, the child was counseled and admonished; her SGL talked with her mother, and later, at the final step in our series of consequences, I participated in a sit-down with her mother and the SGL. Eventually, she stopped coming.

Recruitment Strategies Evolve

As Project Interface gained a reputation for producing competent students, our need to do active recruiting decreased because families started coming to us. Our original student population came from "flatland schools" or "hill schools" in the immediate geographic area. Families who sought us out may have lived in the geographic area, but they sent their children across town to schools thought to offer a better education or to Catholic schools. Newer incoming students tended to come from middle-class families, not the poor families with whom we had started our work. This meant that we had to work to consciously maintain a socioeconomic balance within our student population by continually recruiting in the flatland schools. With the exception of King Estates, we never actively recruited in the hill schools. Recruiting never stops, even when a program has a waiting list. Recruiting is a vital aspect of program outreach and communication; it keeps the work in the public's eyes and hearts.

ENGAGING PROSPECTIVE STUDENTS

Students need their own message specifically framed for them. This section highlights the most important issues to consider when recruiting and talking with students and suggests ways to frame your message to them.

1. Take the developmental stages of students into consideration when framing the recruitment message. A student can write the most touching and sincere statement of interest, be accepted to the program, and still come with no books or materials. I actually said to some of my 7th graders, "Look, let me help you with this. Today is . . . you are . . . this is . . . and you need to remember. . . ." The 7th graders would actually look at me and say, "Oh, okay, Dr. Bouie" or "Oh, yeah, now I remember!" They actually seemed grateful for the point-by-point review. This is an honest error indicative of the developmental stage of the students; it is not deliberately done. The disciplinary process has to provide some room for the benefit of the doubt and for coaching students through their developmental stages.

2. Be conscious of students' prior school experiences, especially if they have not experienced success. The recruitment message has to convey authentic belief in their capacity to succeed academically in order to create a willingness to risk trying again in the face of repeated failure. Student failure in academics is a matter of competence in the subject matter, not of capacity to learn. Failure does not indicate a lack of capacity to succeed and to begin to achieve at exemplary levels. Sharing stories of students who had similar experiences and overcame them can take the sting out of failure and make it safe for students to sincerely try once again.

3. Intentionally address issues that students are beginning to, or have had to, grapple with—such as social class, ethnicity, gender, and language barriers—and talk about how the program can help them overcome these kinds of obstacles. In addition to sharing my failures in mathematics classes, I also shared my behavior problems when I asked students about their citizenship grades. While sharing the fact that I had personally experienced unfair and unjust treatment by teachers and administrators, I could also share about the times they supported me. I shared how I learned to handle unfairness in a way that did not get me into trouble. It was easier for students to absorb what I said when they understood that I had walked in their shoes.

4. Support can come from seemingly unlikely sources. It is helpful to be acquainted with students' favorite television shows, films, recording artists, athletes, other public figures, and, in particular, interviews, articles, or books in which they have expressed their views. While waiting for a plane in the airport, I picked up a book by the Los Angeles rapper Ice-T. It took me a minute to get beyond the profanity and the drama. However, as I read on, I was surprised to see these direct quotes:

> Teachers should be the highest-paid professionals in the country. Without teachers we got nothing.

> . . . kids from the ghetto need to learn how to be less aggressive and how to solve more of their problems with their brains. I want these kids to know the skills they learn *on* the street are as valuable as the skills they learn *off* the street. The person who can merge both of them together the quickest will be the achiever.

> That's the worst thing that can happen to you in the ghetto, to lose all hope.
> (Ice-T & Siegmund, pp. 156, 17, 15)

5. *If parents bring their child to the program, consider strategies to gain the child's interest.* Because students form friendships around perceived common-alities, when unwilling students were dragged into my office by determined parents, I would try to make sure that students from their school were also attending. I also asked the study group leader who would be working with the new student to take a minute to talk with the student and the parent. Another strategy is to have a welcome committee composed of students and turn all new program entrants over to them.

CHAPTER 5

Staff Recruitment, Selection, and Training

> With one person, it is hard to see very far. With two people, you can see a little more. But if you have a whole group of people around really caring about you and telling you, "You are doing the right thing! We want you around! Give us your gifts!" it helps you fulfill your purpose.
> —Sobonfu Some, *The Spirit of Intimacy*

AFTER receiving the endorsement of parents and families, gaining access to students, and generating a flow of applicants, the next essential component of the program is an excellent staff. I learned that a study group leader (SGL) can make or break a learning experience for children, and finding the best available people for the job became my mission.

This chapter discusses the process Project Interface used to recruit, select, and train prospective SGLs for the program. First, I share the working relationship with the Peralta Community College (PCC) District, where we recruited most of our staff for the program. Next, I share the interview process and the questions we used. The "Considerations When Hiring Staff Members" section provides an analysis of issues that became important in the identification and selection of prospective SGLs who would be able to work effectively with our students. Third, I describe the 2-week SGL development process that we designed to prepare for successful work with students during the school year. The 2-week intensive process included learning opportunities for staff in curriculum development, communications with students and families, and orientation planning. A description of the role of SGLs in the pre–academic year student–parent orientation follows discussion of the eight staff training areas. The last section of this chapter highlights issues to consider when planning a staff training session. Appendix Figures D.1, D.2, and D.3 show the SGL training outline and detail the expectations of SGLs. Appendix Figure D.4 shows an example of a science lesson plan created by SGLs.

RECRUITING STUDY GROUP LEADERS

Initially, the grant from the Minority Institutions Science Improvement Program (MISIP) required that all Project Interface SGLs had to be students enrolled in the Peralta Community College system. Juan Vasquez, a counselor at Alameda College, was our initial contact. At our first meeting, he shared with me the process for developing a course that would meet Peralta's requirements for a class of three units of academic credit. He suggested course content and offered to process the papers through the college. I would have to submit a course syllabus and report card grades each semester; in effect, I was an adjunct professor.

In the beginning, Juan recruited PCC prospective SGLs for the program:

> I am going to send you students that I think would do a good job for you and who are good in math and science. But you will have to decide which ones will be good tutors and good team members who will work together. I'm not going to ask them whether they like kids or have had that kind of experience; that's for you to do, but everyone I send you will be doing well in math and science.

He was very straightforward, and his suggestions on the interview process for students proved useful. After a conversation with him, they called me to set up an interview.

I wanted students who were math and science majors, with intentions of transferring to a 4-year college or trade school. They needed to have taken, and done well in, the appropriate math and science classes. They needed a B average or willingness to work toward it as a condition of long-term employment at the program. We agreed that some prior experience working with young people was desirable and that this could be paid or volunteer work. Later on, I developed working relationships with professors in the science and math departments, counselors and staff in the career placement offices, as well as members in the civic, social service, business, and corporate spheres—and all proved to be fruitful sources of recruits. These relationships were so good that I never posted advertisements or notices, or even went onto campuses in order to recruit staff. Telephone meetings with faculty and staff produced solid candidates year after year. Finally, existing staff frequently told their friends and classmates about the program, and this subset of applicants was also an excellent source of new staff.

SELECTION OF SGLs

The Interview

Prospective SGLs completed a written application form and participated in a formal interview with the director. The application form asked questions regarding the following:

- Basic demographic information (address, telephone number, emergency contact)
- Education: high school and college to date
- Math and science classes taken; grades in each class
- Prior work experience
- Long-term academic and career goals
- Volunteer experience
- Community activities and hobbies

Application responses were used to begin the interview and segue into these questions:

1. Tell me a little about yourself, and your experiences in school. Here, I was interested in learning how the applicant thinks about the schooling process and how he or she described experiences in school.

2. It is well known that urban youth are not doing well in school. How do you explain the underachievement? Why do you think they are not doing well in school? I looked for the reasons the applicant provided here. I also explored how he or she thought about the relationships among the child, school, community, and home. I saw a red flag when the applicant saw the child and family as the primary reasons for underachievement and when responses included phrases such as "single-parent families," "they don't want to learn," "sometimes they do not have quiet places to study," or "they are not really motivated." These statements often accompanied low expectations and could indicate an applicant who would experience difficulty in identifying with and building on the strengths of our students and their families.

3. What is your strongest subject? Your weakest subject? What about each do you like and/or dislike? Here, I continued to explore how the applicant thought about school, and I also tried to get a sense of the individual's skill sets as well as perceived strengths and weaknesses. A sense of what each member brought to the table was important for the assembly of a staff that would work together as a closely knit team.

4. Do you consider yourself, or have you ever thought of yourself as, a role model for younger students? Why/why not? Despite the fact that this seems to be a leading question, I always got interesting responses. One applicant, Paul Norris, launched into an impassioned statement about how important it was to be a role model for "the youth" because "they were watching you, whether you knew it or not, and we had an obligation to be there for them and give back to our community." Zealous, yes, but certainly in the right direction.

5. Let's say you asked a student to get to work and the student refused. What would you do? If the applicant stated that he or she would ask the student again, I would ask, *What if the student continued to disrupt the group?* I got an array of different responses. One applicant gave me a blank look and said, "I don't know. Come and tell you, maybe?" Another emphatically said, "I'd call her mother and tell her how her child was behaving. That would take care of it." Still another said, "Well, you know, I'm from this community, and I know a lot of kids, and their older brothers and sisters, and their parents. I would not get a lot of trouble because they know me and they know I know their families." Here I was looking for a willingness on the part of the applicant to assume responsibility for student conduct in the study group.

6. What would you say to a student who has gotten a problem wrong several times and is about to stop trying? I looked for empathy here, the ability to stand in the students' shoes, and the ability to motivate, encourage, and keep a student focused on the work. This was the core of our work, and if an applicant did not respond well to this question, it was doubtful that he or she would be effective with our students.

7. Tell me about your experiences working with young people and what you learned from them. I probed for the kinds of settings in which applicants had worked: Were they structured or unstructured? I wanted to know the kinds of responsibilities they had had in previous experiences, because this could inform their comfort with the level of responsibility that they would have to assume at Project Interface. I tried to discern whether or not their experiences were primarily caretaking jobs or if they also required creativity, imagination, and work with other staff. The experiences shared in response to this question also told me about opportunities they had had to establish and maintain order, earn the respect of students and family members, and develop positive relationships.

8. Let's say one of your students comes to group downcast. After a brief chat, you learn of a serious problem at home. What do you do? I did not expect applicants to field this question comfortably; it is a difficult situation and requires a certain level of experience and maturity to handle well. I was interested in how they responded and the reasons they gave for their responses. There was no right answer because the situation was dependent on a number of variables that would determine the best approach to take. I hoped to hear applicants voice these kinds of considerations, because much of their work would be situational, requiring on-the-spot analysis and response.

9. Tell me about your academic and career goals. I looked for a sense of hope, direction, and goal setting on the applicant's part. I expected some indecision because they were at the beginning of their academic careers; this question provided an opportunity to listen to the way they thought and talked about their aspirations.

10. What are your extracurricular activities and hobbies? Hobbies and outside activities often suggested skill sets and interests that could be used at the program to complement our work. Additionally, if they belonged to organizations or clubs, they might add sources of volunteers or support for the program.

This question set provided a variety of substantive information to use in the decision-making and placement process.

Considerations When Hiring Staff Members

Over time, I learned that, generally, applicants fell into one of four categories. The first category had strong subject-matter competence but was weak in the affective qualities we needed in order to be effective. In spite of their strong GPAs, they lacked empathy, came across as judgmental, and seemed to believe the primary reasons for student failure could be attributed to a lack of parenting and a lack of student desire or ability. The clash of cultures and/or social classes rendered them unable to transfer what they knew:

> Cynthia had taken all the prerequisites for college while in high school, and she had earned a 3.8 her first semester at Peralta. Her content knowledge was excellent, as were her academic and career goals. In the interview, it was clear that she was proud, and rightly so, of her work. When I asked her what she thought she would do with a student who had struggled and failed several times, she said, "I really don't know. I've never had that happen to me. What kind of students will this program be serving? I believe that, if you work really hard, you won't have a problem with the work. Most of the

people I saw that didn't do well in school didn't really study, so that is their fault. I feel if the child tried that many times, then maybe he doesn't belong in a college prep program."

Individuals in this group tended to get frustrated easily with students and, as a result, were not usually successful in connecting with students and their families.

The second group had the beliefs and assumptions we sought but were weak in content. They believed the students could learn and exhibited an obvious comfort level and sense of warmth when talking about the students and the community. They believed that students failed because they needed motivation and someone to inspire them. They usually expressed a desire to give back to the community or to help the young people. All too often, however, they needed a strong support program themselves. This group was able to connect with students and parents but relied on affect and tended to design and deliver weak content:

> Raymond took pride in his ability to relate to the students and bond with them, especially the boys, and we needed that presence at Project Interface. During the interview, I asked him what he would do if a student kept talking after being asked to settle down and get to work. He said he'd pull him aside and have a chat with him. When asked what he would do if that did not work, he stated that he'd try it again, because he would want to keep it between himself and the student, because the parents were "going to come down hard on the kid—especially if it's a little brother—and that's they last thing they need. What he needs is a friend who is always there for him and who will listen to him and understand him. He doesn't need somebody coming down on him for being a kid."

Raymond was emphatic about this and was clearly sincere, and while I appreciated his empathy, I had serious doubts about his willingness to be firm and apply the push when it would be required. Further, his stated assumptions about the child's parents raised a flag for me. How did he know the parents would come down hard on the child? Why would he assume that coming down hard on the child would be inappropriate? Finally, his belief that he was to be the student's friend first and foremost made me uncomfortable. The paradox of working at Project Interface was to learn that, before I could be a friend to my students, I had to have their respect—and that respect had to be established, earned, and maintained. While Raymond had the capacity to learn that lesson, he showed no willingness in the interview to acknowledge its validity, and therefore he would be hard pressed to learn it. Applicants in this group were not usually successful without a willingness to "buckle down" and insist that their students do so as well.

The third group had the potential to become effective at Project Interface. They needed a great deal of hands-on coaching, training, and orientation in either the cognitive or affective area, but they were clearly open, teachable, and willing to work. They could deliver, if coached well. Some of them were weak in the subject-matter area. We could assign them to a general math group or a pre-algebra group. We created contracts covering commitments to study time, increases in their own grade point averages, enrollment in appropriate courses, development of concrete strategies to transfer to a 4-year college, and probation for at least one of their marking periods as a condition of employment. If the applicant was willing to sign the contract, we were willing to hire.

> Harold came to Project Interface with a low grade point average, but on the recommendation of a counselor. We developed a work plan that required him to get assistance with his work and to raise his GPA by the next semester. He was assigned a study group of 7th graders, and his skill with them was undeniable. However, he spent a great deal of time talking and rapping with them, frequently did not administer the weekly quiz, and did not raise his own GPA.

This affable young man was placed on probation but was eventually asked to work elsewhere. How could he exhort junior high school students to study and work hard when he himself did not?

The fourth category of applicants is the group that I loved to see walk through the door. They were fully competent in the subject matter, and they had the expectations and beliefs that fit our mission. They were able to connect with the students, their grade point averages were excellent, their academic goals were positive, and their strategy for future academic work was solidly in place. As with all applicants, they required training, coaching, structure, standards, and direction, but these were young people who were competent and able to connect with students and, probably most important, they were not afraid of a challenge, willing to take risks, not afraid of hard work, and willing to learn what they did not know. They were worth their weight in gold, and they accomplished what some people considered magic and miracles. Their enthusiasm was infectious, and their commitment was inspiring. They soaked up new learning like sponges and grew right before my eyes. They are what made Project Interface fun, challenging, safe, and effective, and, next to the students, they were the very best part of the program for me. I came to look forward to working with them and creating a place where all of us could be a part of something vastly bigger than any one of us.

The percentage of applicants that I would have hired on the spot varied from year to year. As many as 50% or as few as 30% of applicants could fall into the fourth category in any particular year. There were years when I had to look high and low for staff, and others when I had to turn good people away.

TWO-WEEK STAFF TRAINING
AND PROGRAM PREPARATION FOR SGLs

The 2-week intensive was a dress rehearsal of almost every task and interaction an SGL would encounter during the year. It was designed to build on new working relationships, promote the development of task-oriented teams, and prepare the new staff, individually and collectively, for the upcoming year. The goal of the 2-week training was:

> To create competent, highly effective teams where individuals have confidence not only in themselves but in the competence of fellow team members and the collective ability of the group to effectively accomplish the goals of the program in five essential content areas: high expectations, clear structure, nurturing of student growth, rich academic content, and skilled instruction (see the "Creating a Nurturing Program Environment" section of Chapter 8 for expanded descriptions of content areas).

The training was done within a structure of the PI habits of mind—consciousness, intentionality, explicitness, devotion, and security (see the "Creating a Nurturing Program Environment" section of Chapter 8 for expanded descriptions of the PI habits of mind)—and in an atmosphere that encouraged growth and respect for one another as staff members. During the 2-week period SGLs passed through eight training areas, which covered PI's mission, academic program for students, teaching strategies, and communication strategies to use with parents and families. The goal to build an ethos of mutual support and teamwork was integrated throughout the specific training areas. Some of our staff training materials are available in Appendix D. Appendix Figure D.1 is the training outline for the skills areas used to develop PI training areas for SGLs. Appendix Figures D.2 and D.3 SGL show specific expectations of PI staff.

A Teachable Moment

The staff was ethnically and racially diverse; they came with different experiences, perspectives, and values. There were SGLs who had never left

Oakland working alongside staff members from Peru and South Africa; every section of the country was represented, and there were four different languages, three different ethnic groups, an equal number of males and females; they attended 2-year and 4-year colleges and universities and were all at different stages of maturity and development.

As the work progressed, it was gratifying to observe SGLs move beyond their affinity groups of fellow staff members they knew, or liked personally, and transition to task-oriented teams with staff they did not know or gravitate toward naturally. They were in the process of becoming a team that transcended their personal preference and comfort zones with one another to accomplish a common mission.

There were opportunities to explicitly state the principles that would guide us. One SGL, Shawn Moss, shared a recollection with me:

> One day a small group of staff was sitting, talking, and laughing about another staff member's mannerisms. It was almost like what the kids do. At the next group meeting [Dr. Bouie] said, "We don't gossip and talk about one another around here. We just don't. It gets in the way of the work, and it can be personally painful, too." I said to myself, "Whoa, that woman is serious." I just hadn't seen anybody call people out for doing that kind of thing. I know I never gossiped around there, and I worked with everybody. What was a trip is that everyone else did, too.

I was willing to address this because I had seen the consequences of allowing individuals to say that they would not work with people they did not like. Personal prejudices got in the way of the adults' growth. I always wondered how the adults were going to teach children about working in diverse settings when they themselves would hunker down in their respective corners, never to come out, rather than search for ways to accept and become comfortable with different staff members. I knew that students watched adults and that the best way to teach them how to work in diverse settings was to have a staff that actually did it well.

Training area 1: Overview of Project Interface. In the first years, the overview focused on the dreams and hopes that the co-founders of the program had when seeking the funding for Project Interface. As the program developed a track record of effectiveness, staff were asked to build on and continue the record of success. A thorough overview of the program's history, components, participants, structure, and community connections was presented to staff at the beginning of the training.

Returning staff members, former students, volunteers, and board members were all asked to participate in the initial session of the 2-week intensive. One returning SGL shared:

Becoming a part of Project Interface was one of the best things that happened to me. Working here actually helped me want to do better in school and made me realize how important my education is to *me*. I got a lot of help here myself, and I came here thinking that I was going to help the kids. Helping the students helped me see that I really have something to offer, because it was a trip to see them learn and to see that I could reach them. I got such a good feeling watching them grow and seeing their grades go up. Even though the work is hard, it is a good place to be.

One of the program's volunteers encouraged the staff to:

Understand how important what you do is and how many people are watching you. There are many people who believe in you and what you are doing, and who want to see you and your students succeed. They are counting on you to do a good job.

A parent who was invited to attend the opening session stated:

I don't know what I would have done without Project Interface the first year my son was in junior high school. He was starting to think he was grown, and telling me that studying was just not cool. His tutor really turned him around, and a big part of it was seeing a young man that he thought was "cool" telling him how important it was to study and get good grades. I don't know if Brian [the SGL] knew how much of a role model he was for my son.

This kind of sharing was important for the staff because it let them know that they were joining a program with a tradition. They were inspired, and this made them willing to begin to do the hard work in front of them.

Training area 2: Review of course sequence and content, learning grade-level expectations, and proficiency standards. The SGLs were familiar with course sequence and content because they had taken the required courses in high school or were presently enrolled in them at Peralta. They did not know about grade-level expectations and their relation to the design of learning experiences for students. SGLs studied state- and district-level standards to create the Project Interface curriculum. Although at first it seemed to them a daunting task, the SGLs were able work together to combine the state and district standards to create appropriate course content and grade-level pretests. One SGL remembered:

> Dr. Bouie would introduce this stuff to us as if we had been doing it forever. None of us had ever done it, and we weren't sure that we could do it. It was not what we were expecting when we took the job. But she just put it out there so matter of factly that it sounded doable, even though we were scared that we couldn't. . . . She saw that we could do it before we knew we could do it, and she kept at us to make sure we did it. After we realized what we'd done, we began to understand what it was we had to do with the kids—we had to believe in them and hold them to it. After that, we got really involved and began creating on a serious level. . . . We were supporting each other and preparing for the kids.

Because the curriculum project was integrated into team building during the training, SGLs also learned how to support each other and their students during the work with standards. A full description of the curriculum development process and the role of SGLs is included in the "Using State- and District-Mandated Standards" section of Chapter 6.

The Oakland Public Schools published subject-matter grade-level expectations for each subject. After the staff organized themselves into grade-level teams, each team became responsible for being the experts on the competency expectations for their own grade and being familiar with those of the grades before and after their grade level. I explained why they were expected to know content and expectations for not only their own grade but also the ones before and after:

> We know our students are bright, but we also know they come with gaps in their knowledge of mathematics. We are responsible for not only filling in those gaps but also preparing them for entry into college prep classes. This means our students have to catch up on old work, master their present work, and get acquainted with new work. You have to incorporate all three of these phases in your work, and you have to help them understand what you are doing and why.

SGLs were receptive to the challenge and learned to incorporate expectations of adjacent grade levels into the lesson plans for their grade teams successfully. Appendix Figure D.4 shows an example of a standards-based lesson that they created for use during the school year.

Training area 3: Designing math and science learning experiences. At Project Interface SGLs used the standards training to design curriculum components for the program. The SGLs were initially unsure about their ability to design standards-based activities. When given continuous support and time to work together, they discovered that they were capable of creating the necessary curriculum components. Activity development is discussed further in the presentation of curriculum design in Chapter 6.

The climax of the first stage of content development was team presentations to the staff. I observed the SGLs during the presentations. The first team was somewhat self-conscious and hesitant at the beginning of the presentation. They relaxed and gained confidence as they realized fellow team members were supporting them. They observed the rest of the staff listening to them, even jotting notes, and taking them seriously. It was clear that SGLs were beginning to gain respect for one another's competence and creativity and to accept two important truths. First, that they themselves were bright, quick, and capable. Second, that they could be a very powerful, impressive team if they listened to, helped, and supported one another.

Two things were going on simultaneously. The curriculum content was in the process of creation, and a cohesive, mutually supportive work group was developing. The process contributed to the creation of an environment in which staff would be comfortable sharing ideas and strategies and would see themselves as resources for one another.

This process also helped the SGLs learn to hear and accept constructive feedback without becoming defensive and taking it personally. The SGLs learned to reflect on what they were doing, and they learned to hear ideas from one another. They came to see that one person's strength was another's weakness and that they could go to one another for help with problems. Finally, they knew that when they had gotten positive feedback, especially from their peers, they had earned it and their work was of good quality.

It is not necessary to create a curriculum in order to create a cohesive working group. It happened that we had both needs at Project Interface, and the staff involvement in the curriculum development process helped us meet the two goals simultaneously. If the planning process requires that staff work in teams and create ways to make a prepared curriculum relevant to the specific experiences of the children enrolled in the program, it is possible to create a cohesive team without creating a new program-specific curriculum in the way that we did. Collaboratively creating and agreeing on grading standards, learning experiences, and program rules are additional processes that give staff opportunities to work together in ways that foster positive working relationships that transcend personal affinity preferences.

I introduced the SGLs to the concept of designing worksheets for their study groups based on a study group model by Uri Treisman (see Chapter 8 and the "Use of Study Groups" section of Chapter 6 for more on PI's development of a curriculum based on study groups). Worksheets for math consisted of 12 to 15 problems. One-quarter of the problems would cover material that should have been mastered, that every student in the study group should be able to answer correctly. One-quarter of the problems were from material that would be introduced to them later in their present grade or next year in their college prep math class. The remaining half of the problems reflected work students in the group were working on in school.

Study group worksheets for science were developed using the same standards-based approach. Curriculum and activity design for the science content was more difficult to coordinate across schools and grades than math content; it is explained in detail in the "Challenges in the Development of a Science Curriculum" section of Chapter 6.

Various learning group configurations were used to present and teach the worksheet material. SGLs could do the following:

- Present and introduce material themselves
- Assign a student to present material
- Divide the group into teams
- Work with the group as a whole
- Instruct students to work individually

SGLs were encouraged to take the attention span of our students into consideration and change the mode of student work at least once during each hour of the 2-hour afternoon session.

Staff could not begin creating worksheets in earnest until they knew the members of their study groups. They learned relevant information from two other activities: designing grade-level pretests and assigning students to their study groups.

Training area 4. Designing grade-level pretests for orientation. Knowledge of course content and grade-level expectations was needed in order for the staff to design the program pretests administered at the parent–student orientation. The pretests were designed similarly to the study group worksheets, but the problems on them were different. We were interested in assessing the levels of our students at program entry. The SGLs designed pretests to present 20–25 problems covering skills and competencies that students should know if they were performing at or above grade level at the end of the previous year. Pretests gave us a current assessment of student levels and helped us to sort students into study groups appropriately to ensure a complementary range of abilities within each group.

Training area 5. Classroom management. This segment focused on establishing and maintaining a learning environment that included student interaction with one another while maintaining a respectable degree of order and decorum. The topics covered were:

- Program-level rules
- Study group–level rules
- The Series of Consequences
- How to be firm, friendly, and fair

In addition to presentation of information, discussions of the topics, and role-plays with debriefings of the interactions provided ample time for rehearsals and opportunities to refine their new roles as Study Group Leaders. Among the most popular topics were these:

- The opening day
- Talkative students
- Rebellious and disrespectful students
- Gearing up a student who is not working up to capacity because of lack of energy and effort
- Gearing up a student who is not working up to capacity because of repeated failure and discouragement

Training area 6: Working with parents and families. Study group leaders were quick to understand and accept the close working relationships that the program cultivated with parents and families. What troubled them and made them feel insecure was actually talking with and, where necessary, confronting parents about problems they might have with a student. One SGL said to me:

> Dr. Bouie, I have to tell you—I do not even feel like it is right for me to say anything to any of these children's parents. First, they are all older than me, and second, I don't have any children. I do not have the slightest idea about what to say to them.

I told her, and the rest of the staff, that by the time we finished this module, they would talk to parents as comfortably as they talked with one another. I got a room full of doubtful stares, but they indicated that they were willing to at least hear me out. Topics in this module included these:

- Talking and working with parents
- Beginning a relationship with the family

- Reporting good news and updates
- Reporting methods
  The weekly telephone call
  The monthly feedback report
- Parent panel

Training area 7: Papers and forms. Project Interface needed to create policies and procedures, rules, routines, and guidelines, and forms accompanied many of them. Some of the most important were the following:

- The weekly lesson planning sheet (done in duplicate; the SGL and the director have a copy)
- The monthly feedback form (done in triplicate; the SGL, director, and parent have a copy)
- Monthly awards
- Order sheets for materials and supplies
- Timesheets
- Staff, student, and parent contracts (a staff contract is shown in Appendix Figure D.2, and student and parent contracts are shown in Appendix figures B.1 and B.2).

Training area 8: Preparing for orientation. The parent–student orientation was held the Friday before the program began each year. Staff played a large role in preparations and participated fully during the orientation. SGLs were responsible for the following:

- Contacting students and families to confirm attendance at orientation
- Preparing to administer grade-level diagnostic tests at orientation
- Grading pretests and assigning students to study groups
- Preparing a brief, 3-minute self-introduction to be delivered during the orientation

Orientation preparations included creation of the program, which included a description of the work that would be done by students at Project Interface, pretests, and question-and-answer sessions with students and parents. At the orientation SGLs needed to be prepared to state what would happen on opening day and the specifics of how PI would work with students.

The orientation was the first time the group would meet the students as a staff. They worked all day to prepare and get the final details in place and then went home to change clothes and, as one said, "get ourselves together." They transformed themselves from a group of twenty-somethings in jeans,

Birkenstocks, Nikes, and slides into a polished, well-groomed group that emanated an intention to take care of the business at hand. Their anticipation and excitement were palpable, and their eyes were dancing. As they waited for parents and students, some breathed deeply; one rubbed his hands together; another asked a co-worker to remind her of the protocol for administering the pretest.

Training areas 1–8 of the 2-week training session gave the SGLs first-hand experience with the requirements of their primary tasks, and it helped them to gel as a staff and in their subject-matter teams. They developed a sense of their own strengths, weaknesses, and styles—and of those of the collective. As we were preparing last-minute details one year, an SGL said, "I can't believe I've only been working here 2 weeks. I feel like I've been here forever and that I've known you guys all my life!" They had actually seen and experienced one another in action and were ready to start the orientation and the academic year as a cohesive unit, with a sense of mission and anticipation.

Project Interface Orientation

During the orientation, the SGLs took advantage of the opportunity to meet and mingle with parents before the beginning of the program. They were nervous, but they handled themselves well. As they experienced positive responses from parents, it became easier and more comfortable for them. I pointed out to them how well behaved students were around their parents and told them to remember this fact because it would come in handy as the year progressed.

The SGLs took charge of the program when students were asked to leave their parents to take the pretest. Students filed out dutifully with the SGL assigned to guide them to their test-taking site. They entered rooms with pencils and pretests on each desk in preparation for them. Once in the room, they were greeted by another SGL who explained the pretest thoroughly and answered students' questions.

"What if I don't know the answer to these questions? Does that mean I can't come here?"

Typical SGL response: "Of course not. We hope you do not know some of the answers, because we wouldn't be here if you did. We are just using them to get everyone assigned to the right study group."

"Why are we taking this test tonight? Why can't we take it next week when we come here?"

SGL response: "Because we don't want to waste time giving you the test when the program begins. We have to score these tests, put you all in groups, and plan lessons for you. If we wait until you get here, that will waste time we could be using to help you with your school-work and get you ready for the college prep classes you're going to be taking next year."

"Will I be in a group with my friends? I'm not coming if I can't be."

SGL response: "I think that is one of the things you'll like about Project Interface. You will meet new people and make new friends. Not that you don't keep your old friends, but it's fun meeting new ones and you get to do that here."

"I thought I was going to do homework here. We have lots of homework, you know."

SGL response: "You will get help with your homework, but we are not going to spend the whole 2 hours doing it here. That's why they call it *homework*, because you do it at *home*. We read the statements you guys wrote, and you talked about wanting to go to college and so forth. Well, trust me, I'm in college, and you will not believe how much I study. I could not believe how much harder I had to work in college than I did in high school. And you have to work harder in high school than you do in junior high school, so even though we will review homework and even do some of your problems, you will still have to work at home. The things you'll be learning here are study skills, how to organize your papers so that you can find them, and how to do the kinds of problems you have in your homework and problems that you will have in college prep courses. We're working to get you there, and it starts here."

When students completed the pretests and returned to the large group, they found their parents deeply engaged in questions and answers with the staff. As they filed in and joined their parents, we reviewed the evening and shared what students could expect on the first day of the program.

Finally, we formed small groups of parents and students and assigned an SGL to each group. I walked from small group to small group and was impressed with the way the SGLs responded to questions from parents. Parents were involved in all the groups, listening and talking with the SGLs and one another. Students were taking all of this in, and most sat there while their parents and the SGL talked. The orientation served to introduce students and parents to PI staff, introduce the program to students and care-givers, and provide PI with an assessment of students' abilities.

CREATING A STAFF TRAINING SESSION

This section includes suggestions to keep in mind for planning of pre-program staff development.

1. Provide opportunities for staff to get to know each other from the moment they arrive. Once a complete staff was hired, they began working together immediately. I incorporated a lesson I had learned by accident the first year of the program when I was hurriedly completing last-minute details and photocopying materials. Of course the machine was not cooperating with me; it would copy but would not collate the documents. I had stacks of paper on a table instead of completed packets in the room where we would meet as a staff for the first time. I had no choice except to tell them what had happened and ask them to work with me to collate the documents. I told them what the stacks of paper were, how they were organized, and suggested a process for getting them collated. They divided the tasks, organized themselves, and began collating and organizing the documents. When I returned, they were well into the work and had begun to bond as a group. By the time the work was completed, they had chatted comfortably, gotten to know one another, and become a working group. The process was actually an unintended task-oriented icebreaker.

2. Provide opportunities for staff to practice and rehearse with you and each other. Provide feedback and suggestions. This process prepares your staff to accept and appreciate feedback and constructive criticism. College students can be extremely sensitive, and they can have difficulty accepting feedback. The process of role-playing and debriefing scenes where all staff have an opportunity to give and accept reflections shared in the debriefing helps them learn to think about their work, share successes and problems with one another, and learn from senior staff and from each other.

3. Involve clients and volunteers in the process. Clients and volunteers can provide different points of view and reinforce your message. Our staff began to realize through opportunities to interact with guest visitors that clients supported and appreciated the work and that busy people valued it enough to give their time and talents. This gave staff a sense of their part in a larger goal. SGLs were impressed when Dr. Smith Sr. dropped in, and he rarely came without bringing a guest with him; as the year went on, this reinforcement and acknowledgment of hard work helped the staff stay motivated and productive.

4. Get as much time as you can for your training. Two weeks might seem excessive, but our staff benefited tremendously from the time. It conveyed the fact that we felt the work was important and that they deserved the best we could provide.

CHAPTER 6

Designing Challenging Curriculum Content

My daughter was exposed to more schoolwork.
—Project Interface parent

THIS CHAPTER describes our experiences in designing a standards-based curriculum to meet program goals and the academic needs of Project Interface students. It presents our initial discussions and the major obstacles that staff faced in creating a way to structure and present the math and science course content. This chapter also describes how we organized the students into working groups and how we structured lesson activities for the first-day sessions with the students. Appendix Figure E.1 offers a strategy for curriculum development, some specific suggestions to consider, and indicators of effective program implementation. The following chapters on rules and nurture discuss additional program elements and show how we created an environment where students could become successful.

During the design phase the major considerations regarding curriculum at Project Interface were the following:

- The decision of whether to design a "home-grown" curriculum from scratch or use textbooks
- The use of state and district standards
- The level of staff involvement in the curriculum development process and staff training needs
- Resources and materials needed for curriculum design
- Use of a study group method for student learning
- Creation of a process to produce an excellent curriculum.

THE DECISION TO CREATE OUR OWN CURRICULUM

The NCCBPE interviewing committee wanted to know just how I was going to design a math and science program with very little content knowledge of either subject. One member of the panel said:

> We are not interested in a tutorial program where the children go over mathematics that will not get them into college. Your degrees are not in science or mathematics. How are you going to know whether or not the tutors are teaching the right things and that they are accurate?

I was prepared for this question and told them my plan: First, the curriculum would not be a rehash of the general math classes students were already taking. It would not be a one-on-one drill-and-kill tutorial in which students would review material over and over. Second, the curriculum that was offered in the study groups would contain the knowledge and skills students were expected to know at each grade level. Third, it would prepare the students to enroll and succeed in college preparatory classes.

A curriculum that followed a textbook would have been expensive and impractical. At a cost of $40–$50 each and with an enrollment of 60–80 students, textbooks would have been a luxury item. I was convinced that there were ways to spend that amount of money and accomplish more than the purchase of books. Also, since our students attended at least five different schools (and in some years as many as twelve), the logistics of matching students and books was not the best use of time or money. Ultimately, I chose to invest the money in the staff instead of books.

The decision on textbooks also related to the identity of Project Interface. Even though it was an academic enrichment program whose primary mission was to empower students and raise student achievement in school, Project Interface had to have its own style of doing things and a separate identity from school. I discussed this with the NCCBPE engineers, and they agreed that textbooks were problematic. One member stated, "We want the program to be different from school and we really want different results."

The engineers suggested purchasing a prepared curriculum, but they did not know of any that they could recommend, and I did not feel comfortable choosing one. School was out and teachers and others who might have given advice were not available. This meant that we would create our own curriculum. It soon became clear that this was really a gift in disguise. The need created an opportunity to create not only a first-rate curriculum but also a confident, well-prepared, task-oriented staff.

USING STATE- AND DISTRICT-MANDATED STANDARDS

Fortunately for us, in 1983, the state board of education issued the results of the state's Committee on a Master Plan for Excellence in California Schools, *Raising Expectations: Model Graduation Requirements* (California State Board of Education, 1983). The document was released shortly after the influential report *A Nation at Risk* (National Commission on Excellence in Education, 1983), which had been published in April of the same year. This report sparked controversy and action as few others had, and states and school systems across the country responded to the alarm bell it rang.

Raising Expectations noted that "high school graduation requirements were mandated by state law until 1969. Since that time, the requirements [have been] established independently by the state's 382 school districts that maintain high schools. Over the intervening years, local circumstances and financial inequities have resulted in the adoption of disparate standards in which it is possible for students in one district to graduate with 190 units where students in another district needed as many as 265 units" (California State Board of Education, 1983, pp. 33–34).

Raising Expectations presented short, succinct model graduation requirements; acceptable 3-year mathematics sequences; and prerequisites for entry into high school mathematics sequences. It also presented course descriptions and content for all the courses we would teach at Project Interface. I ordered one copy of the report for each staff member, and it became one of our most important reference tools in the creation of the PI course descriptions.

SGLs were quick to absorb the state requirements as a framework for course content and use them in combination with the grade-level proficiency standards issued by the school district. At Project Interface the decision to create our own curriculum meant that SGLs were responsible for creating curriculum material. A significant portion of time during our 2-week training session was allotted for practice in use of the standards. After the process one SGL commented:

> When Dr. Bouie started explaining what she wanted us to do, I sat there and said to myself, "You want us to do what? Where are the textbooks or those pull-out books? I could not believe she expected us to read those [state] standards and go through the [district] proficiency standards, but she did. I looked around, and I was not the only one who was kind of in a state of disbelief, but she kept on going like she was oblivious to it. She constantly asked if there were questions and what we were thinking about the process.

Curriculum development was a challenging task that required a lot of effort from and gave a large degree of responsibility to the SGLs:

> We understood it; we just didn't think we would really have to do all that, and, plus, we were a little intimidated by what she was expecting us to do. I mean, it was a lot of work, and it was pretty serious work, too—we were reading standards books and learning stuff that real teachers learned. It slowly dawned on us that she seriously expected us to do this, and she believed we could do it. She was so straight up about it, like it was important but no big deal—it could be done. Every other word was, "This is going to be really good!" or "You guys are smart, you're good, you can do this," or "Try it, if you have questions, ask me about the process, but not about the content—you guys are the experts there." I mean, she actually had us believing that we could do it at the same time we were sitting saying, "I don't know about this."

The district proficiency standards outlined the specific skills students needed to learn at each grade level; PI used the OPS standards as a guide for goals in our curriculum.

The PI course description was helpful in recruiting sessions with students and in explaining the PI learning process to parents and families. The course description also provided parents and guardians with the information they needed when talking with their children's teachers and counselors to get their children enrolled in college prep courses.

REFINING CONTENT KNOWLEDGE OF MATHEMATICS AND CREATING A STAFF TEAM

There are many ways to develop a curriculum that meets academic standards so that students are achieving at or above grade level. At Project Interface we decided that the SGLs would research and design the curriculum themselves in the context of staff team-building activities during our 2-week staff training session. Designing and structuring the content provided an opportunity for the newly hired staff to learn and work together as a team before the students came on board and to build an ethos of mutual support and teamwork.

Turning the content development over to the SGLs had several benefits for the organization. First, even though they had taken the required classes, they needed to review the course content as it was required at the junior high school level. Second, they needed to become familiar with what students should be able to do at each grade level, along with the sequence of the work within and between grade levels. Finally, they needed ownership of what would be taught, they needed to become a working team, and they needed to believe that they could actually move our students out of general math classes.

During their planning time I heard:

I was in algebra at my school and we didn't cover this!

And:

I was in high school before I got some of this stuff they say you're supposed to have in the 8th and 9th grades!

Through the process of learning to use standards for curriculum development, SGLs became experts on grade-level expectations. They also developed specific knowledge of the gap between expectations and the reality in many schools and were able to connect it to their own experiences.

SGLs told of graduating with a 3.5 GPA or better, feeling well prepared for college, and being devastated when they discovered how little they had actually been taught and how unprepared they were. One SGL shared:

I can still remember how small I felt when I got my first test back. I knew it was going to be covered in red, because I didn't know anything on it, and I had been in geometry in high school, and I had gotten a B. We had not covered half the stuff other people in the class had. I was way behind from the get-go and had to play serious catch-up. It was very bad, and I was in shock. I thought I was ready, but I wasn't.

We knew our middle school students had had similar experiences; our students had received Bs and even As for work that, when compared with other schools—sometimes even within the district—would rate at best a C, and frequently a D. During the curriculum design experience SGLs coined a phrase that became standard jargon at the project: "Walk anywhere work" meant that an A at Project Interface would be an A anywhere.

After the large-group sessions with training on the content and proficiency standards, the staff formed subject-matter teams for math and later for science. Sharon, an SGL attending Merritt Junior College, said:

We are really making sure these kids have what they need, aren't we? Plus, this is like getting a refresher course in math, and that's good for me, because this is foundation, too.

The SGLs had to know and feel comfortable with the big picture: They learned the scope of the subject area to be taught and the appropriate level of competency required at each grade level. The course content refresher was just what they needed to spark their self-confidence and generate enthusiasm. By the end of this phase of the work, SGLs had a solid working knowledge of what students should know at each grade level and the content they would need the following year. They continued with further detail designing learning activities and planning for content to be organized into grading-period, weekly, and daily segments. Appendix Figure E.2 shows an example of the math activities developed by SGLs.

In presentations to their fellow staff members, each team reviewed content and proficiency levels and shared preliminary thoughts about learning experiences they envisioned using to engage students from the very first day of class:

> When we did those first presentations, we were really nervous. It was the first time we'd done anything like this, and we were going to have everybody listen to us. As we started, the other teams listened to us, asked questions, and we could tell they were impressed when we finished. This made the next teams want to do well because they didn't want to look bad. I remember being really impressed with the work we had done. That was when we really started listening to Dr. Bouie and trusting what she said.

Each team received thoughtful, considerate, and challenging feedback that they used to refine their work. The process took a very diverse group of young people who had not known one another and created a cohesive, resourceful group that worked well with one another. Our students saw this; it spoke volumes about celebrating diversity without saying a word about it. See Appendix Figure E.1 for the stages of curriculum development used at Project Interface and additional suggestions.

CHALLENGES IN THE DEVELOPMENT
OF A SCIENCE CURRICULUM

In 1984, Project Interface added science classes 2 days a week, expanding our program from 2 to 4 days per week. The board of directors had two concerns: (1) How would we pay for it? (2) What kind of science could we do in a church fellowship hall with little storage space and no refrigeration except the one in the church kitchen that belonged to the deaconess board?

The science curriculum was problematic from the very beginning and a true labor of love on the part of SGLs for several reasons. First, we had structural problems in determining how we were going to offer the science series to our students. Second, we had facility, space, and storage problems. Third, we had problems coordinating our work with the schools.

When I proposed a science series to the staff, they responded with their usual enthusiasm and creativity, and I remember my shock when several of them walked in with huge college textbooks in chemistry, biology, and physics. I was thrilled with their response, but I had to put the work into perspective for them:

These texts are wonderful, and I'm pleased to see you thinking, but this is way too much for our purposes. We don't need Kreb's cycle; all they need to do is make something change colors, draw a little blood from their fingertips, or make something blow up. We're not talking deep here, guys, we're talking introduction: concepts, basic themes, that kind of thing.

Fortunately, the state frameworks supported this approach; they required a thematic approach to sciences that introduced concepts and preferred depth to breadth of coverage.

The SGLs reviewed the frameworks and retooled their approach, but their enthusiasm and motivation continued, and their creativity came in handy. They continued to develop confidence in their roles and welcomed the challenges in the design of curriculum and activities. One SGL shared:

I remember one [pep talk] that really made us proud and like we were about something: She [Dr. Bouie] said, "If I had to choose between a new facility with the best library out there, with all the equipment with teachers who did not believe the children could learn, and who were not willing to do what it took to connect with the students, and a facility that maybe wasn't the best where the teachers had to make do, but these people believed the kids could do it, and acted like it, and got results, I'd take the second group any day of the week, because the first group isn't going to use any of the equipment anyway, and the second group will think of a way to do it without the equipment." Well, you can imagine how that made us feel. We stopped thinking about what we didn't have and started coming up with all kinds of ideas. After a while, ideas were coming and we almost competed with each other to see who could come up with the best ideas that made the point with the least equipment possible, or stuff we could access. We would tell our teachers what we were doing and ask them for stuff—they almost always gave it to us, and we'd bring it to the program. We got lots of material that way, and we could also order things at the programs—not a lot—but we did have that support from Dr. Bouie.

The SGLs had to create learning experiences that required minimal equipment because we had next to no storage space. Every college in the vicinity must have known what we were doing, because it was rare that a day went by without one SGL or another walking in with something from a laboratory at their school. I can still remember Brandon Mendiola walking in with a balance beam he had secured from the Lawrence Hall of Science. Stephanie Nichols requested yeast and flour—and wound up baking bread in the deaconess' oven. Shawn Anderson put her students' fetal pigs in the church refrigerator; I told her she was on her own with that one and that I would refer Mother Young to her. They buzzed around bouncing ideas off one another, deciding who would be on which of the three teams and which major themes they would present. A sample science lesson plan is included in Appendix Figure D.4.

We began with science during our summer session, which did not have to mirror the curriculum that was being taught in school, and the opening of school posed a problem with our first science series. In keeping with the engineers' desire to have the students exposed to science and math, we structured a yearlong three-part series that featured an overview of concepts and themes in earth, life, and physical sciences. All students, regardless of grade, went through the entire cycle. This was the easiest configuration to develop and implement for the staff. They divided themselves into three teams, planned their 10-week cycle, and ordered and solicited their supplies. They liked it; I liked it. The students and their parents did not like it. The school district offered each science during a specific year—life in 7th, earth in 8th, and physical in 9th grade. The math was intense enough, and adding science that they were not taking in school at the time was too much. They balked:

> I'm not even in biology anymore; I already had it in school. Why do I have to take it over again?

> I can't study all this math, my science at school, and your science, too. It's too much!

> I'm in earth science, not physical science. I need help with that, and we never even talk about it until next quarter. I will flunk out by then!

We reconfigured the science series the next semester. The staff teams remained intact, but students were assigned according to their grade level.

We continued to have problems, even with the retooling, because students attended different schools, used different books, and it was much more difficult to address the different chapters and topics in science than it was in math. The staff's determination and flexibility allowed us to devise a solution that met their goals and the students' concerns. They would use 1 day a week for helping students review major concepts and problems they were having with their homework, and the other day each week they would involve students in an experiment or demonstration that illustrated a theme or concept related to their schoolwork. Occasionally, students would still balk because it was challenging to create experiments that reflected topics that all students were studying.

We also made changes to the staff team approach. The teams reconfigured themselves more along the lines of study groups in which each SGL was responsible for a small group of students, whereas before the entire team worked together to present a lecture, experiment, or demonstration to the large group of students, which was followed by breakout group activities that might or might not include the same students from week to week. Appendix Figure E.1 presents suggestions for effective implementation of curriculum design and indicators of effectiveness.

DESIGNING A TOOL TO ASSESS STUDENT COMPETENCY

The SGLs used the standards training to create pretests to learn what students knew when they entered PI. The pretests were similar to the learning activities. However, they were designed to consist of 20 to 30 items that covered only content that students should have mastered the previous year. Even with intense recruiting, we had no way of knowing which students would enroll or what their competency levels would be. Grade-level pretests provided an opportunity for PI to learn what our students knew, and they provided a way for SGLs to practice application of what they had learned about state and district expectations.

When the pretests were done, each test was revised based on feedback and suggestions from the staff. I also asked an NCCBPE member to review them. He was pleased with the work of the SGLs: "If this is representative of what they [SGLs] know and can do, it looks as if they know their stuff. This is good work." Student scores were used to assign them to the study groups and the SGL they would work with during the school year.

A study group leader suggested that we administer the pretests during the annual parent–student orientation, usually held a week before the program began. This gave the SGLs time to score the pretests and assign students to study groups. I liked this idea because it set a tone of high expectations for student work and effort from the very beginning of their relationship with us.

To prepare for the orientation, SGLs duplicated the tests, sharpened all the No. 2 pencils, gathered scratch paper, and assigned each grade level a room. They decided which staff members would explain the process to the students and their families, who would guide them to their respective rooms, who would be in the rooms to administer and explain the content, purpose, and how we would use the pretest. For a full account of the planning staff did for the orientation session, see the "Project Interface Orientation" section of Chapter 5.

USE OF STUDY GROUPS

At Project Interface, the study groups always included students at different levels of competency in the subject area. We used a continuum of low, medium, and high scores in each of the three grades represented to create a continuum of nine levels and a sorting method that allowed for different levels of subject-matter competency in each study group. A study group could consist of any set of two or three consecutive groups along the continuum of nine score sets. Our study groups combined the following clusters:

- Low-, medium-, and high-scoring 7th graders
- Medium- and high-scoring 7th graders and low-scoring 8th graders who were not enrolled in pre-algebra
- Eighth graders with low, medium, and high scores, along with high-scoring 7th graders
- Eighth graders who were struggling in pre-algebra and high-scoring 7th graders
- Ninth graders enrolled in algebra, or at least pre-algebra, and, in some cases, 8th graders enrolled in algebra or pre-algebra

The permutations are endless, and each year study groups were organized to assure a blend of students across grade and competency levels.

The study group worksheet is a basic curriculum tool that is easily modified to meet specific needs in many subject areas. The worksheet assumes that a heterogeneous group works on a set of 10 to 12 problems or questions where one of them is so simple anyone in the group can answer it and one so difficult that no one can solve it. SGLs designed worksheets to cover material based on the levels of their students.

The study group session was divided into four 25-minute blocks for teaching and learning. SGLs were responsible for leading the study groups and planning activities. The only guidelines were these:

- Vary the mode of instruction within each block, even if the group continued working on the same content.
- Make sure that each session addressed the three spheres of past, present, and future work.
- Make sure that students understood their homework and were able to do it when they got home. Homework was not supposed to be done at Project Interface.
- Answer any and all questions about the work, and address any school-related concerns. The mantra was: "That's why they call it *homework*: It is done at *home*."

Over the years, the guideline for homework at home was a difficult standard to maintain because students would complain, and SGLs would yield. Parents might complain initially, but when we revisited the goals of the program, outlining the long-term implications of the students' development and the consequences of students not learning excellent study skills, we usually got parental support, which helped take pressure off the staff.

It is important to remember that Project Interface was not created to be an after-school homework completion program. Even if our students completed their homework, they would continue enrollment in dead-end math classes that would not prepare them for entry into high school college prep classes. We asked: What is the point of getting an A in general math if it leads nowhere and the student is not equipped mentally and academically to transfer to a college prep class?

If our students were going to make it through college prep classes, they would have to learn how to study and be organized as well as become willing to meet the challenge of doing their best. The study group format, combined with the challenging material developed by the SGLs, provided our students with the chance to experience what would happen when they really worked hard in school and a feel for what it would be like to be on the college prep track.

THE FIRST DAY OF CLASS

All of the 2-week staff training, the curriculum development, and the preparatory work done in the orientation led up to the first day. As the time drew near, we wondered whether we were going to have any students, but we were prepared for a full house. Chairs were lined up in the fellowship hall, classrooms and work areas had been set up, and SGLs had used pretest scores to prepare for the first day of work in study groups. As the students began to trickle in, we realized that the year had started and rehearsal was over.

Once students were settled into their study groups, the SGLs reviewed the program and classroom rules once more and began instruction.

> Good afternoon. My name is Ms. Jones, and I will be working with you this year. This is the pre-algebra study group. After you introduce yourselves to one another, we'll start by reviewing your pretests and finding out where each of you are in school right now. We will do some problems and have a break. During the second half, I'll tell you what a really thorough course in pre-algebra covers, how it relates to what you did last year, and how it will relate to next year. Then we will go back and solve the problems that you are working on in school right now.

I came a little later and observed the group. They were preparing to compare what each of her five students was presently studying. Ms. Jones had drawn three columns on the chalkboard. One was labeled *Easiest*, another *No Problem*, and the third *Do Not Understand*. Standing in front of the board, she said:

> Okay, now I'd like you to look at the homework assignment you have right now. Read all your problems. When you have finished, put at least two problems from the work you are doing in one of the three columns. If you feel you have no problems to put in the last of the columns, do this: Go forward in your book until you find a problem you cannot do.

The students started going through their homework and began to put problems in each of the three columns. After they were done, Ms. Jones said:

> Now, let's look at these problems you all have put up here on the board. These are the questions we are going to discuss after the break.
>   • What is the first thing you notice about the problems in each of the three columns?
>   • What do you see when you look at all three columns as a whole?
>   • How do you think the group could go about helping one another solve these problems?

Ms. Jones had done several things with this simple exercise:

- Generated 45 problems for use in designing her own worksheet using the students' work
- Obtained another quick assessment of her students' strong and weak areas
- Used two different groupings, individual and large group
- Given the students the opportunity for purposeful, task-oriented movement
- Reduced students' self-consciousness or fear by having them share as a group
- Demonstrated that all students had problems that stumped them

Other groups were moving along, but I saw a couple of SGLs who were stumbling.

Next, I entered Ms. Brinker's room. Heather was from South Africa, quite formal, and her accent alone caught the attention of her six 7th graders. She stood primly in front of her group, hands clasped in front of her. She was used to a formal setting where students were attentive, even when bored. She found the energy level of the students, "amazing. They move all the time."

She took a different approach on opening day and asked each student to write down the rule they thought was most important and why. As students wrote, she moved around the room, looking over shoulders and making brief comments. After students finished, she led a discussion using their responses as her material.

Heather then segued into the academic work and asked the six students to form three teams of two people each. After they formed their teams, she asked them to share and compare their homework and their textbooks in pairs, and then to repeat the exercise with one more student. She gave them time to open their books, and then told them to answer these questions:

- Do you have any problems in common?
- Which is the easiest problem in each of the books? Which is the hardest?
- Does one member of the team know how to solve a problem that the other one does not? If so, which problem?

She then made four columns on the board: common problems, easiest problems, most difficult problems, and problems one could solve and the other couldn't. Heather's group was buzzing and had too many side conversations for my taste. I liked her learning activity and shared with her these thoughts:

- The learning experience was a very good way of getting to know her group.
- She needed, however, to give all the directions at one time, ask if everyone was clear, and if necessary go through them again.
- She would have had more time if she had had the columns on the board before the study group began.

I continued to make rounds, establishing a habit that went on throughout the year. After a few weeks, my presence was acknowledged only by a nod from the SGL, who continued on with the work. Students might speak, but they kept working. Sometimes, I'd chat with a student, especially those who were struggling or who might be facing particularly challenging circumstances at the time. I couldn't have a serious conversation on the first day, but I could establish a connection.

The first day closed with students returning to the fellowship hall for the first fireside chat of the year. We closed each day as a large group so that students began to feel a part of the larger program as well as their study groups. I chatted with them about the day and dismissed them. The entire staff took a deep breath. We were all exhausted, but relieved and excited. The first day saw all 60 of our students present. It had gone well, and the problems could wait until tomorrow.

CHAPTER 7

Rules and Consequences, Routines, Rewards, and Rituals

> Keep to the borders of rights and duties. If you learned only rights, it would corrupt you. If you learned only duty without rights, it would debase you. Rise with the sun, and sleep with him, for he is regular.
> —Bouna Bokary Diouara, *Origins*

R ULES, routines, rewards, and rituals were elements of the invisible container that created and maintained the environment of nurture, growth, and achievement at Project Interface. Rules and the accompanying Series of Consequences created norms and articulated our expectations for behavior. Routines provided stability and consistency and also helped establish trust among staff, students, and families. Rewards acknowledged and celebrated effort and achievement. Finally, rituals made values, beliefs, and aspirations visible and tangible for the eyes to see and the heart to feel.

A program with no rules or follow-through invites chaos and breeds inconsistent, arbitrary behavior on the part of staff and students. A system with no routines breeds uncertainty, insecurity, and a sense of isolation from others. If there are no rewards, effort becomes drudgery, achievement goes unrecognized, and motivation flags. A program without rituals has no soul, no heart, no vision, and it cannot inspire perseverance through difficulty.

Rules, routines, rewards, and rituals at Project Interface were a tightly woven, interrelated, interdependent, and mutually supportive set of strands that supported our mission and helped us support one another. We could not have survived without establishing and maintaining a clear set of rules for behavior and following through on the consequences for breaking them. In the first section of this chapter, I describe the process we used to create our rules and consequences. In the second, I describe the routines that created a stable and secure structure for students and staff as well as continuity for the project. In the third I share the rewards we developed to reinforce positive change in student engagement and improved academic performance, and in the fourth I share how our rituals conveyed our values and helped create and sustain our community.

Appendix F includes additional details in the PI rules and Series of Consequences (Appendix Figure F.1) and a chart of characteristics and behaviors that explains how we addressed student needs for structure in the program (Appendix Figure F.2).

RULES AND THE SERIES OF CONSEQUENCES

Development of Rules and Consequences with Students

When we first developed the rules, I contacted as many students as I could find during the summer and asked them to meet me at my office because I needed some help; about six of them came through and gathered around my desk in anticipation of the conversation. I said to them: "I'm going to make some rules to have before the program begins, and your ideas are important. What do you think the rules should be? One replied:

No fighting and hitting.

Another:

Respect everybody.

And another added:

Be on time.

With some prompting, they also added:

Bring everything you need.
Try hard.
Don't call people names or make fun of anyone.

I said, "These are excellent. Now what should we do if you guys act up? I think the first time you break a rule, we should call your parents right then." I didn't really mean this, but it was a negotiating ploy that I knew I would need.

We eventually agreed that parents would be called the second time. From the beginning, I thought that calling the second time would be appropriate, but I knew if I started there, the students would argue, even if they felt it was fair, just because they liked to disagree. I had to give them some room to express their opinions and negotiate before we came to a conclusion.

Another rule provided a teachable moment during our rules development session. There was a suggestion to add "no disrespect" to the list. Our students soon discovered that this was not as simple and self-evident as some of them had thought. In fact, one student said, "We already got not calling people names. What else are you talking about?" Amber said, "You can disrespect somebody and not even open your mouth. You know they're dissing you, and they know you know, and they haven't said one word to you."

Amber made an excellent point, but John was not convinced:

Well, how are you gonna go around and check on people's actions all day? You can't do that, plus, what if you say I disrespected you, and I didn't mean to, and didn't even know I was doing it. Everybody makes mistakes. You're gonna call me out for a honest mistake? That's wrong. You can't do that. That's not fair.

Amber had to admit that John's hypothetical exchange was true and could happen, but she came back with:

Well, yes, and the person shouldn't get punished if it's a mistake, but I'm talkin' about the for-real ones—like when somebody throws you that look—you know that's disrespect, and people will fight you for lookin' at 'em funny. Sometimes you can not even know you're lookin' at 'em like that and they *still* get mad.

John felt vindicated and said:

For real, for real. That's what I'm talking about. You gonna have a rule sayin' people can't look at each other? That's crazy, but I do know what you mean. My mother, and you, too, Dr. Bouie, can stop people right where they're standin' just lookin' at 'em, so I know you right, but still but I do not see how you can tell people not to look at other people.

The group concluded that the rule should be left in, even though it could create situations that might be hard to decide. The students had excellent points, because students often say nothing out loud but communicate disrespect of one another and adults nonverbally in many subtle and not-so-subtle ways.

This rule acknowledged the reality that communication occurs at a number of different levels, in many modes, and that disrespect means many different things to different people. While the rule was not to be interpreted as attempting to "stop people from looking at each other," it did put everyone on notice that consideration, tact, and support of one another were expected behaviors. Inclusion of this rule also served as an excellent way to re-create the discussion the students had had in my office during the summer with all of the students when the program began.

I also asked parents to review the *rules* and the *Series of Consequences*. They were pleased to have been asked and agreed with all of them, especially the *Second Calling Rule*. One parent emphatically said, "As far as I'm concerned, you can call me the first time. I'm not sending her down there to play. She already plays too much. You do what you have to do, Dr. Bouie."

Those were sweet words to hear from a parent. They meant that I was seen and experienced as a member of the child's extended family and had all the rights and responsibilities that a biological parent would have in relation to caring for the child. Andrew Billingsley (1992) characterizes this relationship as "fictive kin," one of several different types of family in the Black community. With endorsements like the one above, we felt confident that the rules and Series of Consequences were considered to be fair, even if strict, to the student. And we knew that parents had enough trust and confidence in us to reinforce us when we needed their support.

Project Interface Rules

The result of the rules development process was a clear and concise set of agreed-upon rules, with little room for misinterpretation. The rules were a tool that helped staff, students, and families establish an environment of mutual respect and set expectations for focused learning. The PI set of rules is shown in Appendix Figure F.1. The rules that students and I developed in the summer of 1982 guided the project with no changes until 1987, when two additional rules were added. Appendix Figure F.2 shows the approach we used to incorporate students' developmental stages into our strategies for working with them.

Steps in the Series of Consequences

The Series of Consequences used at Project Interface was adopted from Nick Caputi's work, a process that consisted of a series of escalating, sequential steps in dealing with student misconduct. When Project Interface began, Nick Caputi was a consultant to the National School Resource Center, where he presented material from his experiences as a principal in the Oakland Public Schools. The Series of Consequences was useful because it allowed staff to exercise both sides of the disciplinary coin: being tough and tender.

First infraction: The student and tutor will talk to discuss the situation and hopefully resolve the problem. The student has a conversation with an SGL or another staff member. This step acknowledges the concern, brought up by John in the rules development process, that students might forget to do something and that they needed a chance before parents were called.

A student might say:

> You're saying you're stopping me because I don't have pencils and paper? I loaned my pencil to my friend and he didn't give it back to me, an' I forgot to ask my mother to buy me some paper.

My response would be:

> Wait, let's back up a little. You're busy, right? Got a lot going on. [Of course the student would agree, making the point seem even more trivial.] I know how you feel. I do, too. There are at least 60 of you guys here, about 15 SGLs, I am working on a proposal, and it's my night to pick my son up from school. Do you really think I would be spending time talking to you about this pencil if it were not important? Now, think about it: What does it mean if you are going someplace 4 days a week for 2 hours a day to prepare yourself for high school and college and you come with no pencil, no paper, and no book? What does that suggest? Tell me: What does that say?

> That it's not important.

I would continue to prompt:

> Good, go on.

> That I'm too busy and got a lot on my mind.

> Okay, you're too busy to think about your future, but go on: What else does it say?

> That I'm not thinking.

> Keep going.

> That I'm not prepared.

> And?

> That I'm gonna have to borrow one from somebody and they may not have one, or they could say no.

Now, let me ask you, would you go to a barber who told you, "Oh, man, I'm sorry I can't cut your hair today and give you that fade in time for the party you're trying to get your mother to let you go to because that girl you like is going to be there and you want to look good."? Would you?

No.

And what did you tell me you wanted to study when you went to college?

I wanted to be a doctor.

And you're going to go to surgery with no pencil?

Okay, Dr. Bouie, I'll remember.

This is a good thing. Now what is the next thing you will make me do if we have this conversation again?

Call my mother.

Good, now get to your group. I'll see you at break.

The conversation in step 1 allowed us to demonstrate that we would follow through, even on little things that, at first glance, might appear petty or unimportant.

Second infraction: The student's parent will be called on the very next infraction. Students did not want us to call their parents or caregivers, but their early involvement helped stop many small misbehaviors from snowballing into serious issues. Early intervention also prevented students from forming bad habits that would then have to be unlearned. I learned that it was in the student's best interest to involve parents early, despite protests and sometimes tears. I drew from a previous experience at an elementary school where I had observed five 6th-grade girls teasing some 1st-grade students unmercifully. I was incensed and said, "You all come with me right now, and we have some phone calls to make."

They shrugged and did their best to appear nonchalant as they sashayed into the office. I lined them up to make the calls. The first child called her mother. I said, "Mrs. Wilson? Hello. I'm Dr. Bouie, and I have your daughter on the line." Her daughter got on the telephone and told her mother the reason for the phone call. After she finished, she shrugged. Her friend behind her asked, "You in trouble?" She replied, "Humph, no." I said, "Oh, really? You just talked to your mother, and you're not in trouble? Call her back."

She balked but made the call. I said, "Mrs. Wilson, just now, when Jamilla got off the phone, her friend asked whether she was in trouble and she said, 'Humph, no.'" Mrs. Wilson said, "What? She said what? Put her back on the phone."

By time that conversation was over, Jamilla was shedding tears that she hoped would gain her sympathy, support, and some slack. Her friend was outmaneuvered and suddenly quiet. I said to her, "Now it's your turn." All of a sudden, with two telephone calls, I had five subdued, apologetic girls in front of me as opposed to five belligerent rebels daring me to confront them on their behavior. This stood me in good stead at Project Interface, because I learned students would often attempt to stop us from communicating by acting as if they didn't care or by saying that their parents didn't care.

I also learned that I did not have to accept "My mother's not home." I observed that different caregivers might arrive to pick a student up, attend a meeting, or drop something off for a student. I heard conversations such as, "I stayed over my aunt's/grandmother's/cousin's house last night" or "I left my homework at my big sister's house." I concluded that telephone calls to any of these adults would accomplish the mission. I learned to respond to "My mother's not at home" with, "Fine, no problem; call any adult in your family network. I need to talk with someone whose house you stay at on a regular basis." I was always able to talk with an adult in the child's nuclear or extended family.

When speaking with extended family members, I simply shared who I was and said, "Would you tell so-and-so's mother or primary caregiver I needed to connect because we want to keep him on the beam." Or "I called you because this is important. So-and-so said her mother wasn't home, and I needed to talk with somebody grown." This usually got a chuckle and a promise to relay the message. Usually the adult had met me or knew of the program. The call also resulted in a chastised student who learned the hard way that we meant what we said and that we would follow through on the phone call. This first call was often effective. If not, we advanced to the third step in the process.

Third infraction: The tutor, the director, and the student will meet. In many cases we were successful in establishing behavior contracts with students or discovering particular challenges during our conversation that we were able to help a student resolve. In some cases, parents or caregivers also participated in this step. At the end of step 3 we had a written commitment sheet, which detailed the resolution discussed and the responsibilities of each person present. The student, SGL, director, and parent received a copy. We were committed to working with students and their families. However, we did not allow students who would not respond to the rigor, nurture, and tenets of the program to continue to disrupt it. When we were unable to resolve problems during step 3, students went to step 4—and sometimes beyond, ultimately leaving Project Interface. One such student was Marcus, a bright and already streetwise 7th grader.

During the step 3 conference with Marcus, we developed a behavior contract stipulating that his attendance would improve at Project Interface and at school. Marcus had demonstrated an intense desire to learn the skills that would lead to college prep classes. However, he was unable to work within the structure that Project Interface provided. We knew that he needed extra support to succeed and did our best to provide that support.

We worked with Marcus day and night. We talked with his mother and his grandmother. We went to his home many times, tracked him down, showed up at his school, and met with school personnel. We had community people talk with him. We wrote behavior contract after contract. Nothing worked. He cut school; he cut Interface; and he was running with older boys who were bad company. When he came to Interface, he did not work. Eventually he stopped coming.

From time to time, I got reports on him. Marcus was kicked out of school. Marcus was on the streets. Marcus was in a gang. Marcus was up to no good. I was saddened and frustrated; one failure can dampen any number of successes.

Several years later, Marcus came to visit me. He was enrolled at Morehouse College on a scholarship and was on his way. Of course, I wanted to know what had happened. What had "happened" was the Omega Boys' Club, established and implemented by Joseph Marshall (1996). Omega was designed to recruit, enroll, and work with young men whom the streets had captured. Joe's target population was former gang members. Former gang members were definitely beyond the scope of Project Interface.

Marcus had believed that Project Interface was lightweight; he felt he was too advanced and too cool for us, and maybe he was. He needed something else at that time in his life, and Omega was there to meet him. Even though Marcus—and other students—did not stick with PI, the very fact that he returned to say thank you and check in let me know that we had had an impact—and possibly had prepared him for Joe and the Omegas. I learned that Tom Peters's (1982) exhortation to "stick to the knitting"—meaning to discover what you do and do it to the very best of your ability—was sound advice. Our mission precluded working with students whose needs outstripped our capacity.

Fourth infraction: A conference with the student, his or her parent(s), the tutor, and the director will be held. A student has had plenty of notice by the time a request for an on-site meeting with caregivers is made. The first three steps—dialogue, telephone call home, and a written commitment between student and staff—had been completed, along with weekly touching-base calls and a monthly feedback sheet that recorded progress, effort, and behavior. When the third step was insufficient, we were forced to come to the unpleasant realization that perhaps a student did not belong at Project Interface. These conferences were held when a student, and in some cases the adults who participated, did not uphold the agreements in the written commitment sheet generated in Step 3. I would begin the conference by sharing the student's behavior, which led to a problem-solving session with the student and parent.

Something powerful happened to young people when they saw educators and caregivers aligned with one another, a new experience for some of our students. The on-site parent conference was usually the day of reckoning and had the tone of a come-to-Jesus meeting, with the student facing parents and program staff united by concern about effort and behavior. When students experienced this step, they finally had to accept the reality that significant adults in their lives were holding them accountable for their performance in school.

During these conferences, I focused strictly on the student's behavior and actions. I described what I had seen:

> During the large-group assembly Billy was talking and making jokes while the guest was speaking. He does not bring his books and homework from school, and he disrupts his study group by entertaining everyone.

The parent sat listening to the list and looking at the student. There were typically two ways for the conversation to go. Either the caregiver asked, "Is this true?" and, on confirmation, began the come-to-Jesus phase of the meeting. The other response was a forlorn sigh, "I don't know what to do with her; she's getting on my last nerve, and I'm tired." I preferred the first response because it required less work and the student's behavior changed much more quickly.

The second response required that I begin the come-to-Jesus conversation by asking the student:

> What do you do that is more important than doing well in school and getting an education? If there is something that takes precedence, please tell me. Is there something anywhere in your life that is getting in the way of you focusing on your schoolwork?

Frequently, students shared concerns or problems, such as missing an absent parent or family member, feeling overwhelmed by responsibilities at home for siblings and chores, or feeling uncomfortable with relationships with adults or peers at school. This often led to communication and sharing between the parent and the student. Often, the situation did not change, but the presence and active listening of caregivers communicated support, understanding, concern, and love.

We started the problem-solving process by asking, "What do you need to do differently to improve this situation?" Typical student responses included "pay attention in class more," or "turn my homework in," or "turn the television off," or "think before I speak," or "tell my mother/father/ caregiver about the situation instead of handling it myself." The student then wrote these observations on paper.

Next, we asked parents how they would support these efforts and what the consequences would be if the student failed to live up to his or her end of the bargain. Finally, we asked how we could support the student at Project Interface. All comments were written down, and everyone signed and received a copy: the student, the parent, the study group leader, and the director. The structure of the Series of Consequences allowed for inclusion and investigation of personal problems, family issues, or other serious challenges that our students faced.

Sometimes the process led to a much deeper conversation, as was the case with Jason's conference. Jason's grandmother had ridden several buses to attend the conference, and the three of us went into the church sanctuary to talk when she arrived. He shared his grief around the fact that he had not seen his mother and that his father was in prison. He lamented not having money for things like the kids he saw on TV. He was lonely, brokenhearted, and felt the abandonment that comes when significant adults are absent. His tears fell silently as he tried to stop them. I shared with him my own experiences and asked him:

- Do you have everything you need right now: food, shelter, and clothing? Do you have some of the things you want? You do not have all of them, true, but do you have any of the things you want?
- Does your father write to you? And I know he wants you to do well, doesn't he? Does he say this in the letters, and do you write him back?
- Is there anyone, anyone at all in your life right now that you know loves you and is there for you?

He turned to his grandmother, an elderly woman with gnarled hands. He bent back, and looked at her as if it was the first time he had ever seen her. He hugged her and stopped weeping. I shared:

One thing I have learned, and one thing I see right now, is love is always present. It may not be coming from who you want it to sometimes, but it is always present. It will be there for you if you let it.

The three of us went on to talk about why getting an education was important, how he could do better in school, and what he could do about his feelings about the absence of his father and mother. Of course, none of this could change the circumstances Jason faced. The face-to-face conference provided an opportunity to talk, listen, and give one another the courage and support to go on with life. This conference gave Jason an opportunity to receive support from caring adults and to claim responsibility for doing his schoolwork, listening to his grandmother, and no longer acting out. His grandmother received support and reinforcement as she assumed the task of caring for her grandchild. I was able to connect by sharing from my own experience. After a bit, I asked him what he thought his father would want for him if he were there: "Would your father want you not doing well, worrying your grandmother and not respecting her?" Jason acknowledged that in spite of everything, his father "wanted him to do good, and not to be in prison."

These meetings were not always so poignant. More often the meetings were a matter of presenting a united front to the child and following the problem-solving process. We usually had no other conferences of this sort with a child and family.

Over time, we learned that Project Interface could be effective in reaching and working with the majority of students in Oakland's middle schools, regardless of their family composition, socioeconomic level, and other characteristics thought to influence student engagement, effort, and achievement.

But not all. Marcus had been at a critical point in his life, and we realized that he being poor and living at the apartments on 66th Avenue and East 14th Street were not necessarily the primary reason why he was beyond our reach. I have seen and worked with students like Marcus who lived in the hills of Oakland as well as in the flatlands. Both environments produced students with whom we could not connect, and who needed another program.

ROUTINES

The set of routines that we followed at Project Interface provided scaffolds for stability, consistency, and the experience of a safe place.

Administrative and Staff Routines

We understood that our students had six or seven different teachers, six or seven different sets of classroom rules, in some cases huge new facilities to navigate with only 5 minutes between classes, and heavy books that must not be lost. Project Interface was yet another place where demands were being made; the least we could do was to be consistent in the requests we made of students. All staff members were trained to implement the same set of rules using the same process:

- First, a conversation with the SGL and student
- Second, a call home to the caregiver
- Third, a meeting with the SGL, student, and director
- Fourth, if steps 1–3 failed, a face-to-face meeting with the student, parent(s), and director, sometimes resulting in departure from the program.

All students could expect the exact same rules and consequences from any staff member.

Program Routines to Begin the Year

Project Interface routines began during the annual student–parent orientation (discussed in depth in the "Project Interface Orientation" section of Chapter 5), where we celebrated the accomplishments of students, explained rules, presented basic program information, and administered pretests. The first day of the program included reintroductions of returning students and their accomplishments, reintroductions of SGLs, and repetition of program rules.

Acknowledgment of student success. At the beginning of each year, we paid particular attention to returning students who had entered college prep classes at their home schools. It was important to show students living proof that movement into college prep courses had been and could be achieved. Returning students proved that students could make the transition from general math to college preparatory math classes or that they could turn failure in a college prep class into an A or a B. Each student was asked to stand up and share his or her name and school and the transfer he or she had made.

Repetition of project interface rules. On the first day of the program, I called the group of 60 students to order and welcomed them once again. Even though we had reviewed the rules, the Series of Consequences, and the reasons for the rules at the orientation, we reviewed them again, because middle school students forget things, and it is important to repeat them. I engaged them in a question-and-answer session by asking whether anyone remembered a rule, and then asking another student to explain why the rule was important, and still another to state one of the steps in the Series of Consequences. The group was able to state the rules, reasons for them, and Series of Consequences steps.

When the study groups assembled, the rules, reasons, and Series of Consequences were reviewed again with the SGLs, who had been coached in facilitating discussions, as well as in study group routines and management. Some SGLs thought this was overkill, but I shared my reasons with students and staff:

> Students here come from at least five different schools. Every school has its own rules and its own way of doing things that you are used to. At the end of the day, we're asking you to work hard, pay attention, meet new people, and learn new things. In addition, I realize you have other important things on your minds. Like whether Julio is going to call you or you're going to call. Like what will your buddies say if they find out you're trying to talk to that girl you swore you hated. Then there are the new jeans with holes in them already that you have to talk about with your mom, auntie, pops, older brother, or anyone else who will listen to you. And you had time to eat a lot of sugar on the way down here. Are these things true? Are those enough reasons to repeat the rules over and over again?

They had to admit that there were valid reasons for repetition of the rules. The tone set at the start, especially in study groups, was the tone likely to prevail throughout the year.

Staff received continued support and time to ensure a consistent program for students during the weekly staff and planning meeting. Students did not attend the program on Fridays. The SGLs planned for the upcoming week and completed administrative tasks, and I facilitated a staff meeting and problem-solving session with them.

Year-Long Program Routines

Project Interface used additional routines to establish a consistent environment.

Daily Break. The break consisted of 10 minutes of running around the church grounds between classes each day.

The Daily Fireside Chat. At the end of the day, the students would convene with me in a large group for a chat on a current topic of interest.

Daily Attendance. Students were accounted for each day. If they were absent, the study group leader or I called home.

The Weekly Study Group Quiz. A math quiz was administered every Thursday.

The Weekly Touching-Base Call. SGLs called home once a week with a quick progress report.

The Bimonthly Guest Speakers. Guest speakers, called role models and mentors, came on alternate Thursdays.

The Monthly Feedback Form. The monthly feedback form summarized attendance, effort, academic achievement, and citizenship; it was completed in triplicate for the SGL, parent, and director.

The Monthly Awards Ceremony. Each month PI recognized students for attendance, effort, academic achievement, and citizenship.

The Quarterly Newsletter. The quarterly newsletter highlighted program, staff, and student accomplishments.

REWARDS

Our rewards system included five possible ribbons that could be earned by students on a monthly basis. Awards were presented to students during the monthly awards ceremony and acknowledged in the Project Interface newsletter.

This was one of the few times students were recognized for effort and academic achievement instead of athletics or entertainment activities. Parents told us that ribbons were on bedroom walls, on refrigerator doors, and inside school lockers. Often guest speakers would help present the monthly awards, adding a special touch to the event, in the following five categories:

1. *Attendance*: Earning this ribbon required no more than one absence per month.
2. *Effort*: SGLs nominated students from their math and science groups who had exhibited increased effort and were making steady progress. This was an important award because it helped students understand and experience first hand the fruits of their own consistency and

perseverance. They began to see for themselves that they could indeed become excellent students.

3. *Citizenship*: SGLs acknowledged improved behavior, support of fellow study-group members, and positive group participation.

4. *Academic achievement*: This ribbon was awarded to students who had earned 90 or better on each of the weekly quizzes during the month. Students were understandably proud when they received this ribbon.

5. *The Over Excellence Award*: Many students earned all four ribbons; this ribbon acknowledged that achievement.

RITUALS

Project Interface used two rituals, the annual convocation and the annual awards banquet, to express gratitude and appreciation to staff, to children, and for community support.

The Annual Convocation

The annual convocation brought together the entire Project Interface family and was the most overtly spiritual of all our activities. Our intent was to ground the program's mission in a cultural tradition where a sense of calling, service, and responsibility to family, community, and one another was stressed. The convocation consecrated the year ahead and sought the spiritual and moral support of the program's immediate and extended communities as PI began its work for the year.

The convocation was a formal ceremony held at Allen Temple. Students led the processional, followed by staff and then board members. The senior pastor made remarks, students and staff were introduced, and a prayer was offered for an auspicious school year. Each SGL's introduction included a brief statement about his or her academic and career paths. Returning students who had successfully transferred from general math classes to college preparatory math and science classes were given special recognition, along with their family members. Parents were asked to stand to tremendous applause, as were corporate and individual donors. The program ended with refreshments, prepared and organized by parents, in the church fellowship hall.

In addition to community building for the program itself, the convocation was an excellent opportunity to involve extended family and community members, invite potential donors and supporters, and increase the program's presence in the larger community.

The Annual Awards Banquet

The convocation began the year and the awards banquet ended the year. Both were spiritual, celebratory, and rooted in the tradition of program constituents. Here, too, students, parents, and board members were featured prominently on the program. The formal program involved a procession of students and staff, the singing of "Lift Ev'ry Voice and Sing," an invocation, and a guest speaker. The board chair and the director awarded each student a certificate of completion and achievement. The annual awards banquet provided an opportunity for students and staff to celebrate the year and to receive acknowledgement, encouragement, and praise from their families, the board, and the larger community.

By using a consistent system of *rules, routines, rewards, and rituals*, in a setting that was already familiar and resonant with deep meaning to students and families, PI worked to create an emotional connection that allowed students to bond with the program and staff so that we were like extended family members. This meant that parents returned our calls, believed us when we had to report bad news, and felt affirmed in their belief in their children when we reported good news. They showed up to support our work—and for the simple pleasure of seeing their children engaged in meaningful work with other students. Parents allowed us to have conversations about what they were doing at home and acted on our suggestions for changes. Adults would see to it that students did what was asked of them at home because they knew that the positive changes they saw in their children's engagement and academic achievement were the result of a partnership of caring adults. Students saw this, too, and extended the regard they had for their families to us.

CHAPTER 8

Pedagogy as the Nurture
and Cultivation of Students

Every blade of grass has its own angel hovering over it, whispering,
"grow, grow, grow."

—The Talmud

T
HE MOST important work at Project Interface was done in the study
groups. Every other program component was designed to reinforce
or complement the processes that occurred during the study group
work sessions, where students were able to shed misperceptions about themselves and find their ability to learn and achieve. The context of our approach
was firmly rooted in an understanding of the students and their community
and a firm belief that they could succeed. We learned that the way we did
things was as important as, if not more important than, what we taught.

This chapter begins with the community context in which we were able
to provide a nurturing pedagogical approach. It then provides examples of
student engagement in interactive study groups and of the significant relationships that students developed with SGLs and program staff. It also describes how four additional program elements reinforced the instruction and
nurturing process in the study groups: dealing with prejudice, teachable
moments, fireside chats, and role models. The chapter includes excerpts of
interviews conducted by the research team of UC Berkeley's Task Force on
Black Student Eligibility (University of California, 1989a). It also includes
excerpts from interviews that I conducted during and after my participation
in the Project Interface program.

Appendix G answers the questions we heard so frequently: How do you
get them to come every day? How do you motivate them? How do you explain what you do?" Appendix Figure G.1 shows Bloom's Taxonomy of the
Affective Domain, a familiar construct, and corresponding strategies that PI
developed to address varying levels of student engagement. The taxonomy
provides a continuum that assesses the extent to which students are at-
titudinally and emotionally engaged with their education. An accurate assessment of students' scores on standardized tests and report card grades was

important, but insufficient for our complete work. Over time, I learned it was necessary to be able to consciously and intentionally intuit and determine where students were on an *emotional* continuum and to devise strategies that might be effective at various stages. Without an equally astute sense of their affective and emotional engagement, we would never get to the academic work necessary to achieve our goals. Bloom's Taxonomy categories are accompanied by strategies used at PI that can be effective with students at different points along the continuum.

Descriptions of the study group formation process and examples of sessions on the first day of class can be found in the "Use of Study Groups" and "The First Day of Class" sections of Chapter 6. Elements of nurture also appear in Chapters 7 and 9 in discussions of our commitment to work with parents and families through the Series of Consequences to support and encourage student achievement.

A NURTURING PEDAGOGICAL ENVIRONMENT

Our relation to the larger community was an important context for the nurturing approach that we created in the program environment for students at Project Interface. We also built into the program a significant level of involvement from parents and other adults known to our children, and this was an important part of student success.

Our Notion of Community: Family, Equality, Potential

The Black church, the community's oldest institution, first articulated the beliefs of family, community, and equality, which undergirded the organizations, professional societies, and self-help groups that the early church housed and nurtured to maturity. The church had always represented and created an extended family and community for its members, and it had traditionally opened that hand to anyone needing the help it might provide. The concept of family as an inclusive model, irrespective of bloodlines, referred to individuals related not only biologically but also by shared interests, needs, and relationships. This sense of family is based on the view that all adults are responsible for children and that children belong to all caring adults.

In the church, the principle of equality meant that everyone, regardless of social status or past failings, was inherently valuable and had the potential to become somebody. The church created a sense of belonging among a diverse group of people by creating an environment that nurtured its members and encouraged members to nurture and support one another. "The ground is level at the foot of the cross" is a frequently heard folk saying that summarizes this value.

The church and the engineers believed in the *capacity* of the young people to achieve and acknowledged their responsibility to help them in any way they could. In spite of students' apparent lack of interest and actual failure in school, the Project Interface proposal writers believed that the students had the promise and the potential to do better in school and had the ability to achieve as well as any other students if given the proper environment.

The founding beliefs of Project Interface matched those held by members of the community. When asked about the long-term benefit from the program for her child, one parent stated that, "For my son, it was exposure to African American people who understood math. That was so surprising to him."

Project Interface provided students with the skills and experiences they needed to succeed, because, all too often, they did not get them anywhere else. One student, Ayana Cooper, said:

> The program gave me what school did not. It gave me a chance to experience the real world up close. It taught me about taking care of business and staying on task. That carried over from school to a way of life for me. I was given a lot of motivation by the tutors, and I was taught a lot of interaction skills with other children and my teachers.

The core beliefs that define family as community, and community as family, were instructive for everyone. A former board member, Lynn Cerda, stated that working on the board made her "aware of the tremendous need among students in the public schools and . . . the positive impact the program had on the students." The core beliefs of ATBC and NCCBPE were made manifest in their determination to focus on the strengths of children and families along with their ability to address inequity in educational outcomes by creating an environment for promise and potential to grow. This notion of community formed a basis for the Project Interface mission and activities.

Creating a Nurturing Program Environment

Our expectation and belief that our students would do well was the bedrock on which everything else was built. Though intangible, this belief could be felt and observed. The UC Berkeley research team reported that:

> Not one of the respondents [in their survey of SGLs and administrative staff] attributed students' low achievement to the individual student or to their parents. (University of California, 1989a, p. 49)

Acknowledgment of structural and systemic barriers to student learning was crucial.

At PI we were determined that lack of achievement could be overcome with the proper support, environment, and expectations. After some years of experience with the program, I began to see the Project Interface approach as characterized by five key elements:

- *High expectations*: The staff were guided by the absolute certainty that the students could learn and achieve as well as students anywhere.
- *Clear structure*: The students had rules and consequences, routines, rewards, and rituals.
- *High nurture*: Our staff deliberately developed close bonds with students, their extended family networks, and the organizations in the neighborhoods where they lived.
- *Rich content*: A rigorous curriculum is the backbone of the program, which incorporated state standards as described in the California State Frameworks for Math and Science and in Oakland Public School District grade-level proficiency standards.
- *Skilled instruction*: Our staff were particularly trained to meet the developmental needs of middle school students.

The habits of mind that guided the implementation of the work can be described in five major ways:

- *Consciousness*: We attuned ourselves to the implications of the students' repeated experiences of failure, the biases they often confronted in the larger society, and the consistent reflection on our own perceptions of and expectations for students so as to avoid communicating overtly or implicitly negative expectations and perceptions about their potential, capacity, and their families and community.
- *Intentionality*: Every act was deliberate and intended to produce a specific result. We avoided reacting in the moment to students or their behavior.
- *Explicitness*: Students and extended family were told not only what and how but also why each directive was important. We consistently took time to explain, review, repeat, and communicate in ways that resonated with students and families.
- *Devotion*: I was continually inspired by the authenticity of the SGLs and volunteers at Project Interface; "determination" does not convey the extent to which the work was experienced as an important opportunity to serve, give back, and make a genuine difference in the lives of our students. Staff approached the work not as a job, but as an integral expression of who they were and desired to be.

- *Secure*: Staff were confident and assured that they were doing the right thing when holding students to high standards, even when students were frustrated, discouraged, and recalcitrant. Staff stood by the hard calls because they learned that their own efforts on behalf of the students eventually bore fruit.

Together these key elements and habits of mind formed the framework that led from our consistent and strong beliefs that children could achieve to actual success for students.

Vatrice Lanier, a board member who worked at Xerox and attended Allen Temple, frequently dropped in to visit and talk with students and staff. She described the program environment:

Project Interface was about changing people's lives, and it did. It touched the children's spirits and their minds, because it made them believe they could learn. . . . The program and the staff and everybody else nurtured that belief until it bore fruit. For me, imparting that belief that they could learn was the most powerful thing, because that vision helped the children to see what they could not yet see—the adults saw it for them, and everybody at Project Interface—all of the adults believed they could do it, and told them so . . . at [Project] Interface, there was a spirit, an energy there that nurtured the children's ability and willingness to perform.

The sincere and strong belief that children could achieve was foundational, and it was palpable throughout the program.

Vatrice Lanier also described the impact that PI could have on an individual child:

It helped my stepdaughter—she actually looked forward to going to Project Interface. Here the child was out here in California with us on summer vacation and she's getting up 5 days a week to go to Project Interface—and actually looking forward to it! I couldn't believe it! I know it helped her, because the program had her doing things she had never done before, and she saw herself really doing them. Her self-confidence soared.

She saw the impact of the program environment on a child in the form of increased engagement and academic progress, and other student and parent participants also noticed these effects.

A student who had returned to the program said:

> I like the fact that I can get extra help, prepare for exams, and
> socialize with other students. I like the fact that I can help other kids
> learn. My grades have gone up. I have changed my attitude about
> studying biology. I get good grades in geometry.
>   The program helps you focus on math and get your homework
> done. When you are surrounded by everyone who's achieving, it
> makes you want to achieve, too. At first I wanted to be a lawyer;
> now I want to be a biochemist—to study oncology—cancer. My
> study skills have improved. When I got to higher math classes—
> algebra, geometry—it was a breeze because I had already been
> exposed to so much here. My godbrother owns a computer store; he
> influenced my college plans a lot. So did Dr. Wilson. She always tries
> to help me out; she talks with me about college—it seemed like her
> favorite expression was "stay on course."

Students felt the effects of the environment and found it to be conducive to
learning. They saw their own progress, and their parents agreed with them.
    A parent interviewed by one of the researchers describes the environ-
ment her son experienced at Project Interface:

> It was a very positive atmosphere for Michael, which of course made
> me feel comfortable, because he was in a learning environment.
> Michael loved being there, and I really liked the fact that the staff
> was concerned.

The combination of structure and nurture was critical to the engagement
of students, from which their future success and their ability to succeed
would grow.

A Community of Proactive, Nurturing Adults

The structure and nurture that adults provided were essential elements of
the learning environment. One student shared with researchers the effect the
program had on him. When Reginald came to the project, he made it clear
that he was there because his parents wanted him there—and for no other
reason. He was a freshman in high school when researchers from the University of California at Berkeley interviewed him and other students at Project
Interface. He told them, "Before I started here, I was a real disciplinary problem. I didn't respect teachers or anybody" (quoted in University of Califor-

nia, 1989a, p. 56). He also stated, "I like the tutors and the atmosphere. The people are friendly, and you can come to them when you need help. . . . My grades have improved, and I am getting along a lot better with people" (quoted in University of California, 1989a, p. 56).

Reginald responded well to the partnership developed between the program and his parents to encourage, support, and insist on academic achievement. This young man is the same student whose home I visited in Chapter 7. His mother, he, and I had a 2-hour conversation in the family's living room at their home in the Oakland hills. It required time, patience, and mutual support between adults at home and at Project Interface to provide the nurture needed to root Reginald in the program. This support allowed him to experience nurture *and* structure in the form of consistently enforced rules, personal attention, and high standards set by adults who cared about him. The mutual reinforcement adults provided each other helped the parents to hold firm, and it helped program staff to continue working with Reginald without giving up, because we had the reinforcement of his parents. The fact that other adults were reiterating the same themes he heard at home and at school meant that the adults surrounding him were saying the same thing in different ways.

A consistent message articulated vertically and horizontally throughout the program by staff and administrators alike was a solid element of the program, and it was included in staff training. I frequently reminded staff that although no individual staff member could reach each child in each particular situation, as a team we had the ability to connect with almost every single student who walked through the doors of Project Interface. The administrative assistant's desk turned out to be a favorite stopping place for several children. Everywhere students turned, they received encouragement and affirmation that they could achieve. Refusal to let students perform below their ability and insistence on their attempts to meet their potential were constant elements of the continual process of nurturing at PI to help students reach the point where they would be fully motivated by their own experiences of academic success.

STUDENT ENGAGEMENT IN INTERACTIVE STUDY GROUPS

The study group instruction process combined student engagement with high and consistent expectations of students. Study groups were designed to provide engaging opportunities where students couldn't help becoming interested and involved in their own learning.

The UC Berkeley report described the interaction in a science lesson:

> It is 4:30 P.M., and 15 students are divided between three tutors [SGLs] in the Life Sciences class; they are all sharing the large fellowship hall. The lesson is "The Scientific Method." Each group of five students is working on a different experiment. The group that was observed tested what would happen when different chemicals were added to purple cabbage water. Each student in the small group selected a different chemical, and each obtained a different reaction. They bubbled with enthusiasm as they got feedback from the SGL and each another and as they compared their respective results. The other two groups were conducting different experiments, after which each group presented its work to their peers and fielded questions from SGLs and other students. (Frye et al., pp. 47–48)

Researchers, students, parents, and board members noted the level of interaction in study group sessions.

Doreen Anthony-Bullock served on the board and remembered, "We often stopped by the program and sat in on the study groups ourselves." She described what she observed in a math study group:

> Somebody would throw something out—a question, a problem or something, and everybody responded. It was an interactive process where the kids and the SGL responded. . . . The kids were actually engaged and not sitting around waiting to be instructed.

Lessons requiring real student engagement and activity were a new experience for many of our students, and the Project Interface setting encouraged them to participate fully. The active engagement of students through SGL activity design and instruction was an essential building block of academic success for students. The group interaction also provided a setting for positive academic relationships among students to occur.

Positive Academic Interactions with Other Students

Middle school students are loyal to one another to a fault, and we tried to use those relationships to our advantage as well as theirs. While students took weekly quizzes individually, they rarely competed on a one-to-one basis. Instead, competition was always one study *group* against another *group*. They were willing to go up against another group without mercy; and win or lose, the group took ownership for the experience, not the individual. One of the themes that emerged from the interviews conducted by UC Berkeley was the nature of students' relationships to one another:

The UC Berkeley researchers found that:

> These students are not only motivated by tutors, they are also motivated by their peers. They experience themselves as being in the midst of achievers which serves first to identify them as an achiever and second to reinforce behavior that accompanies achieving. . . . Students were asked whether they experienced any negative pressure from nonparticipating peers as a consequence of attending Interface and whether attending Interface prevents them from participating in other activities. . . . Students were overwhelmingly positive about their experiences at Interface and denied experiencing any negative pressure from their friends. (University of California, 1989a, pp. 58, 70)

A student's reflection illustrated the value of other students:

> My tutor was Ms. Price. She was great. She cared, and that meant a lot. My friend Akicia also made the experience good.

We incorporated the developmental characteristics of students into our instructional design, and the role that staff played in designing appropriate activities to engage students encouraged students to believe in themselves and each other.

SIGNIFICANT RELATIONSHIPS WITH SGLs

Long before students internalized the beliefs and skills they learned at Project Interface, they experienced significant relationships with staff members. Often, it was these relationships with individual staff members that held students long enough for the transformative process to take hold within them. In many cases this relationship began when students saw the investment made by SGLs in the learning process.

SGL Investment in Student Learning

The success that students experienced at Project Interface was a very important motivator, and it was one that students recognized themselves. Each of the 13 students interviewed by the UC Berkeley team told a similar story:

- Their grades had improved.
- Their attitude about learning had changed—they now liked learning.
- They liked being in the company of achievers.
- Their study skills had improved.
- They now worked harder.

Some of them reported being "turned on" to math and science. However, this success was the result of many days of hard work, and it was hard for students to see their future success when they first entered Project Interface.

Many of the students had not been eager to engage in learning at the time of their initial enrollment in the program. The work that occurred at Project Interface *before* students reached the point where they were motivated by experiences of their own success was our first challenge. A common theme that emerged in student interviews with UC Berkeley researchers was the way that students experienced the commitment made by SGLs to the student learning experience. The UC Berkeley report states that "the students perceive the tutors as being invested in their success, and they seem to appreciate the almost personal relationship they have with tutors" (University of California, 1989a, p. 57). A student gave an example of this point: "I like that they try to help you. They don't want you to fail. I have changed in my work, I have gotten better test scores, and I am doing more work than I used to do" (quoted in University of California, 1989a, p. 57).

The dedication of the SGLs impacted this student's willingness to take risks and work hard. The SGLs showed that they valued students by refusing to let them remain unengaged, and students responded positively to the continued efforts of SGLs to engage them in learning activities.

The program and the work of SGLs also affected student perceptions of their learning abilities. The UC Berkeley report also states:

> The subjective data strongly suggest that Interface is having a positive impact on its students' perceptions of their own abilities, self-expectations, and aspirations. (University of California, 1989a, p. 57)

Janice reflected on her science SGL:

> I struggled with physics, and Ms. Scott, another one of my SGLs, did hands-on demonstrations to help me conceptualize the work. She used everyday examples of things I was familiar with, and she'd say, "It's like this," and she just would not give up. I'd leave class and when I came back 2 days later, she'd say, "I thought about something else, and here's another way to come at that problem."

Angela, a student who went on to become an SGL, talked about her math study group experience:

> When I was a student, I remember in my study group that we raised our hands a lot and we did a lot of troubleshooting. We would have a lesson or go over something on the board—there was a lot of board

work. Mr. Wajid would put the problem on the board and talk it through out loud. It was very visual. I think he figured that if one of us was having problems with it, then all of us would or had at some point. We would go over the problems several times; I don't remember us ever leaving with a problem unsolved. We paid attention—in the study group, you just paid more attention. We got individual help when we needed it. Mr. Wajid would hang in there with us till we got it.

SGLs did not give up on their beliefs in students' abilities, and they required students to be actively engaged in the learning process. Students learned that support would be there from SGLs throughout the process. The experience of ongoing nurture and cultivation of themselves as learners was an important element on the path to success and achievement, and our staff's commitment to student success correlated with the students' willingness to try and to take risks.

Development of Significant Student and Staff Relationships

I will always remember Janice, who came in as an 8th grader in true form: hands on hip, popping gum, rolling her eyes at me and her mother, and daring me to speak to her. She attended Montera Junior High School, far away from the East Oakland flatlands, and was clearly enrolled because her mother wanted her there, and she became one of our best students. She reflected back on what attracted her to the program in an interview:

> The SGLs were closer in age to me and that was a help, because by the time you are a teenager, you resent an adult telling you what to do. But she was only 4 or 5 years older than me, and it was clear, even to me, that they were trying to teach us because they knew it was in our best interests. I felt like they were on my level and I could relate to them. When you're a teenager, you don't want to hear from your parents, but the SGLs and Dr. Bouie were saying the same things that my mother was saying.

Another student emphasized the relationships that developed with the SGLs:

> I liked the fact that the college students took on roles as mentors with us. They were very encouraging, and I developed a big sister relationship with some of them. They were good at motivating me because they would share their experiences with me, and even

though I knew they cared about me, they never spared the work. Sometimes I would groan and resist, and act like I was not going to work that day, but they just stood firm. I guess they knew that I really liked them and didn't want to disappoint them. The program taught me self-determination and not to let obstacles get in my way.

Some students mentioned their relationship with the director:

Dr. Bouie had a no-nonsense attitude with regard to education. She had the program well organized. She was also motivating, encouraging, and very hands-on. She acknowledged my achievements, and we still keep in contact today—she has been there for me since day one.

Another young woman reflected:

I had the closest relationship with Dr. Bouie. She was just so cool and down to earth; she was so goal- and business-oriented. She had an open-door policy and was always there for me. She never judged or criticized me. I always felt that I could go to her and talk about anything. Her presence was powerful, and she really stood out.

This same child's parent shared this comment with me:

You know how they get, Anne—I was an older mom, and I never even told her how old I was because they didn't have anything to say to "old people" and didn't half listen, but they loved you, and what was so beautiful is you were saying the same thing I was saying, but she could hear it from you! It was really a blessing.

Parents recognized the relationships that their students had with program staff, and they developed their own relationships with staff. The role that parents played in supporting their children and the program is discussed in detail in Chapter 9.

NURTURE THROUGH ELEMENTS
OF PROGRAM STRUCTURE

The study group learning process was reinforced by several other program components. Some of the reinforcement came from daily interactions, addressing prejudice, and teachable moments, and some came through formally scheduled fireside chats and guest speakers.

Counseling and Coaching to Deal with Prejudice

The issues of prejudice, gender, language, and race had to be addressed because students were not subtle in sharing their daily experiences and observations. They would often come to me or another staff member saying that a teacher was prejudiced or "She doesn't like me because I'm Black." The staff could not simply turn a deaf ear and dismiss these concerns. Instead, we learned to probe the experiences they shared to help students see their part in the matter. Equally important, they had to learn how to deal with bias and low expectations in proactive ways.

For example, a young, enthusiastic, bespectacled, and bright-eyed 7th grader came to me and shared that he felt the teacher was prejudiced. I asked him what happened that made him feel like that. He said, "I always raise my hand, and she never calls on me. She won't explain the work to me, and she won't answer any of my questions." I told him that those were legitimate concerns, whatever the reason for the teacher's behavior.

I asked whether he'd told his parents. He said he hadn't. I suggested that he tell them his experiences and that his mother be the one to deal with that situation, not him—this was a matter for an adult to handle, one of the reasons he had grown people in his life.

Finally, I told him I'd talk to his mother if he wanted me to. He said he would like me to call her, and I did. I suggested she pay the teacher a visit, because, prejudiced or not, the teacher was doing her son a disservice. Any 7th-grade boy who is complaining because the "teacher wouldn't call on me" was to be praised, encouraged, and given some support. The parent made an appointment to talk with the teacher. The next thing I knew, the young man came in, beaming, to say that things are better in his math class.

We saw ourselves as advocates for our students, and we also believed that it was essential that they examine themselves and their contribution to any situation. One student complained about a "mean" teacher. I asked to see one of her papers. She handed me a crumpled assignment with no date, no subject line, no title, and no name on it. I asked her how she would feel if she had to read 250 papers that looked like that every day. The student looked at me as if I had lost my mind, but she understood how she would feel reading 250 papers like that every week.

We could not be effective in our mission to help students succeed academically unless we were prepared to help them with challenges they encountered along the way.

Teachable Moments

There were incidents and events that occurred during the days and weeks of the program that were seized upon and used because they spoke to the hearts and minds of our students. These moments could not be planned; they presented themselves, and if we were fortunate, we recognized them for what they were and used them. They served as a way to connect what students knew and believed with what we were presenting to them. Teachable moments encouraged, challenged, or illustrated a point to students.

During the onslaught of crack invading the East Oakland community, gunshots and drive-bys were almost a weekly occurrence. The community was shattered and torn, and our children were not spared. I was making my usual rounds during the break, chatting and talking with staff and students, when I noticed one of my students looking downcast and dejected. Chantel was usually bubbly and smiling, but that day there were no smiles. Break was ending, and I suggested we take a short walk to finish the conversation. As we walked around the block, she told me the reason for her gloom:

> One of my good friends got shot in a drive-by shooting over the weekend. He was just standing there when this car drove up. They were not even looking for him; they were gunning for somebody else, and he was in the way.

As we walked, she talked and I listened—I finally asked whether she had been talking about this so that her feelings could flow. She said that she had, but she had stopped because she was tired of talking and it didn't do any good anyway. She continued, "I don't know why God took him. He was my friend, and he wasn't doin' anything. I really miss my friend, and I feel scared now, I really do."

It might not have meant anything to this student to say, "Sometimes life is not fair, and we do not understand why some things happen." But it was possible to connect with this child by asking if she had ever heard the old people in church saying, "We'll understand better by and by" or "If it hadn't been for the Lord, I would not have made it." She said, "Yes, yes I have." I continued:

> Well, this is what they are talking about, right here, what you are going through now. Nobody can explain it or make the pain go away. You have to feel it, and cry, and be mad sometimes, but you can't hold it in or it will poison you. It does do good to talk. People can tell you how they got through a bad time, what they do to feel safe, and people can help you—I heard someone say trouble shared is cut in half; happy times shared make them double. Now, what do you think your friend would want you to do? Go around not talking, carrying everything around, depressed, and messing up in school?

She replied, "No. He would want me to go on, I know he would. He was glad I was comin' here." I continued:

> This is a horrible thing we're going through and it hurts me to my heart that my kids are dealing with this madness; none of you is over 15, and you're already on the firing line. It makes me feel helpless and afraid, too, but I am still going to show up anyhow. Going on doesn't mean you don't feel bad, it just means that sometimes it's hard and heavy, and you still have to do what you gotta do—for yourself and to honor your friend.

As we rounded the corner, she was not her usual self, but she was not the gloomy child whose countenance had struck me and caused me to stop. At that afternoon's fireside chat, I pursued this issue with the whole group.

Fireside Chats

At the end of each day, all students and SGLs gathered in the fellowship hall. We could have simply dismissed them, but convening them gave them an opportunity to experience being a member of a large group of students who were all about achievement. It created a sense of belonging and community while serving as a time for conversation and reflection. During fireside chats, in small groups, or individually, students often raised the issues of prejudice and unfairness. They had a great deal to say about the fact that things are not fair. It would have been useless at best and patronizing at worst for me to deny that unfairness and prejudice existed. I couldn't be honest and shy away from the subject. In fact, I sometimes raised it—usually in the context of explaining why it was necessary to be prepared, to be confident, to persevere in spite of negativity, and to not let anyone deter them from their goals.

The day of my conversation with Chantel, I began the fireside chat by asking how many students had lost a friend or knew someone who had lost a friend. Nearly two-thirds of my students' hands went up. When I asked how many were talking about this with someone, about half of the hands stayed up. I repeated the thoughts I had shared with Chantel earlier, and students shared theirs as well. The messages of perseverance in spite of painful situations and drawing upon the cultural traditions of the students enabled us to take a painful situation and draw the potential lessons from it.

The fireside chat was one of the many situations that allowed us to talk with students in much the same way that a member of the extended biological family or fictive kin would. In all my years at Project Interface, just one parent expressed discomfort with our taking on hard issues with the children. One of the benefits of close relationships with students' caregivers was that they began to see us as supportive of their children academically—and also supportive of them in their challenge to impart values and strength to their children.

We told students that they would not always be judged by the content of their character and that there would always be people who might doubt them and their abilities. We would then return to the refrain of why we worked hard, pushed and prepared them, so that they would be able to know that they were capable and not doubt themselves. I would often state that this was why we wanted them to do their best, to know that they could do as well as students anywhere, and that we expected them to do so.

The discussions could be intense and compelling, and we didn't always agree. The discussions were necessary to help students deal with complex issues they saw or experienced every day without shying away from hard questions or hard answers. The essential message was that they had to be strong, courageous, and competent, and that they could prevail in the face of prejudice.

Guest Speakers as Role Models and Mentors

Twice a month, guest speakers, called role models, made presentations to students and staff. They shared hope and experiences and provided encouragement, powerfully reinforcing the program, caregivers, and community. Role models were primarily scientists and engineers, but they came from all walks of life and represented an array of professions and ethnic groups.

Role models were asked to cover these topics when they spoke to our students:

- Their successes and failures
- Hard times that they had experienced and weathered
- The academic preparation needed for their career
- Their accomplishments and aspirations they were presently working toward
- Their salary range, the opportunities in their careers for advancement, and different kinds of jobs
- How the work students were doing prepared them for high school, college, and a career

Role models were especially helpful in reinforcing positive coping skills and aspirations in three key areas: difficult family situations, ethnicity and race, and athletics.

One of our former students had this to say about the guest speakers:

> It was really important for other people like Dr. Bouie and the guest
> speakers to be saying what my mom was saying. I remember someone
> telling me about flunking and how he didn't let that stop him. It was
> hard for me to make the translation from going to school and having
> a career. Hearing their experiences made it seem attainable to me.
> Two things helped me. First, they said they did it, and I could do it,
> and then they told us how they did it.
>
> Also, when Kevin Anderson came, it was really amazing to me
> that someone from corporate America would come and work at
> Interface for 9 months. I didn't see people coming back to help us,
> and it made me realize that people who had achieved success were
> still committed to helping us.

Students felt a direct impact from the presentation of real-life success stories.

Money was the second-highest attention-getting topic. We began to include it in our preparation packet for guest speakers because, without fail, students asked them about money, whether they had ever failed in school, and whether or not they were married. When an engineer matter of factly told students they could earn $30,000 to $50,000 right out of college, all of a sudden doing well in math seemed like a really good idea to the students.

An individual visiting our program lamented the materialism of the students and their inability to defer gratification for future rewards. She stated that she tried to encourage students to love learning for learning's sake, not for material gains. I responded with two thoughts:

> First, if money will motivate my students to work hard enough to
> earn an A or a B in a college prep course when they were earning Ds
> and Fs in a general math class, so be it. If a high salary or fancy car
> will make them willing to buckle down and put forth the effort
> necessary to transfer from a "consumer math class," fine. The
> experience of success comes after the work, not before it. In fact, they
> are not going to "love" learning until they experience some success at
> learning—in school.
>
> Second, the entire society is materialistic. Why pick on students
> and their parents?

The money hook was very effective for getting students' attention; they were also able to benefit from other areas of the presentations.

We asked the role models to address issues around race and gender. A person who shared the ethnic heritage of our students was a powerful example and had a profound impact. Hearing from a person who had experiences with prejudice, discrimination, and sometimes also poverty or foster care gave students hope that they, too, could overcome their own circumstances and experiences.

On the other hand, we learned that guest speakers from other ethnic groups had powerful stories that also resonated with our students. First, many of them had personal experiences that were just as painful or difficult as those many of our students faced. They heard firsthand that they were not the only ones facing troubles. Second, our students heard the same high expectations, exhortations to work hard, encouragement, and visions for a bright future that every guest speaker shared.

In a city where race was often a highly charged issue, it was important that students knew there were people who looked like them and who did not look like them who were concerned about them. We often told our students that everyone who looks like you is not necessarily your friend, and everyone who does not look like you is not necessarily your enemy. Guest speakers put real faces and people to those words, and they had an impact that words alone could not have had.

Mack Hay of PG&E was one of our most compelling speakers. He shared about his childhood, telling the students it was very difficult and that he began to work at about the same age many of them had. He said his friend Buddy worked with him at a grueling, low-level job—shoveling chicken manure to be made into fertilizer. He reminisced that his buddy drank and skipped school, would miss work, and was almost fired. He said he used to try to tell his friend that they could make it out if they tried. Mack was a natural storyteller who ended the vignette in a dramatic tone, looking straight into the students' eyes: "You know, all these years later, you know where Buddy is right now? Shoveling chicken manure. You don't want to wind up like Buddy." I frequently heard students quoting or talking about speakers long after their visit.

One of the speakers who addressed athletics in a powerful manner was Jim Brovelli, head coach at the University of San Francisco. Coach Brovelli came through rush-hour traffic to speak with our students, and he did not come alone. He knew the students well enough to know what would have an impact on them and get them to listen.

The tall, handsome African American student who accompanied him walked in on crutches. The team's star, he was out for the season with a broken ankle. The young man spoke eloquently about the need to have a solid academic record, even if you were a basketball star, because anything could happen, and he pointed to the cast on his leg and the crutches he used.

He had their complete attention, they were spellbound, and many of the students wore very somber expressions by the end of the hour.

One year at the annual awards banquet, all three student speakers, unprompted by anyone in the program, mentioned the role models in their remarks. One said, "We had role models come talk to us about staying in school." Another said, "People who are really busy and working very hard took time to come and talk with us." And the third said, "When that man said 'You have to decide whether or not you are serious,' for the first time I really understood what they were all talking about."

I learned a very important lesson from my students. They essentially told me that they were listening, watching, and paying attention—even when I thought they were not.

CHAPTER 9

Mutually Supportive Relationships with Parents and Families

We think it is uncivilized for a child to have only two parents.
—Aboriginal folk saying

The program is helpful in teaching me how to help my child advance better and at a steady pace.
—Project Interface parent

THIS chapter describes the way Project Interface worked with parents and extended family members to establish and maintain mutually supportive relationships. These relationships were a crucial element of success for the students and the program. In this chapter, I share the reasons parents enrolled their children in Project Interface, our initial interactions with parents, their perceptions of the program, and the way we implemented our strategy for work with families. I also include discussions of commitments from our parent contract, the dynamics of typical parent conferences, and the ways that parents were involved in the day-to-day life of the program.

Each year, Project Interface enrolled between 50 and 80 middle school students who attended 4 days each week from late September to late May to study mathematics and science for 2 hours each day. The fact that they remained through the challenges and achieved success was a testament to the involvement and commitment of our parents. Without their endorsement and reinforcement, our students would not have stayed long enough to see for themselves the miraculous changes in their academic achievement.

Appendix Figure G.1 explains in detail our strategies for development of relationships with parents and caregivers.

PHASE I: EARNING CREDIBILITY AND ENDORSEMENT

The Families at Project Interface

Andrew Billingsley (1992) identified three general categories of Black families: nuclear, extended, and augmented. The first category, nuclear families, is composed of a husband and wife and their own children, with no other members present. The second category, extended families, include other relatives or in-laws of the family head who share the same household with nuclear family members. The third category, augmented families, includes members not related to the family head who share the same household living arrangements with the nuclear family.

In addition, within the framework of these three categories, Billingsley (1968) identified and described 12 different types in the basic typology of Black family structures. The 12 types included variations on the composition of family members who lived in a household and which family member headed the household. A cursory review of our students reveals that all of the categories, and quite possibly all 12 of the types, were represented in our student body.

In 1988–1989, 66 students were enrolled; there were 36 boys and 29 girls. They were all African American. Thirty (46%) were from two-parent households; 27 (42%) came from single-parent homes (this figure is almost twice as large as in the wider Elmhurst community, where only 27% of the homes were headed by a single parent). Nine students (12%) lived with a grandparent or other relative.

Although Project Interface did not collect income data, occupations were listed on the student application form. There were a total of 85 parents and caregivers. Five (6%) were retired or otherwise at home and not in the labor pool; 24 (27%) were in managerial and professional occupations; 21 (24%) were in technical, sales, or administrative support occupations; 15 (17%) were in service occupations; 16 (19%) were craftspersons or laborers; and 4 (5%) were unemployed. In summary, almost a third of our students had parents who were white-collar professionals, and nearly two-thirds came from blue-collar, or working-class, homes.

Our acknowledgment and validation of various family structures was a building block of our program, without which we could not have successfully helped many of our students prepare for academic success in the college prep track.

Reasons Parents Enrolled Their Children in Project Interface

Parents frequently cited "declining grades" or "academic difficulty" as reasons for enrolling their children in Project Interface. Parents interviewed by staff at the University of California at Berkeley felt that their children were not being "challenged" or "stimulated" at school, and the parents felt the children "needed a different kind of environment" (University of California, 1989a, pp. 64–65). One parent said that her daughter's math teacher, who was an Allen Temple member, suggested the program as a "preventative measure" and another source of support. The report also found that parents wanted their children to go to college, and perceived Project Interface as a reinforcement to affirm and support their aspirations for their children (University of California, 1989a).

Communication with Families

Initial Contact with Parents

Initially, the first point of contact was the school, where I worked with the counselors to identify students. The first meeting with students always included mention of their parents and the fact that, if selected, students could not enroll in the program unless their parent, or another adult in their extended family network, attended the parent–student orientation.

Our relationship with parents began when we received completed student applications. The telephone call to talk with them would determine whether the student enrolled and remained in our program. The obvious reason for the telephone call was to confirm consent for the child's enrollment and adult attendance at the student–parent orientation. The equally important unstated purpose of the call was to begin a relationship with the significant adults in the lives of our students. Even though the SGLs never developed a uniform script—they were too creative and individually different for that—they followed a template of points to be made during the conversation:

- Thank the parent for supporting the child's interest and following through in completing and submitting the application
- Confirm that the student is still interested
- Confirm that the parent is still supportive
- Probe for any questions the parent may have and answer them (e.g., goals, requirements, hours, structure, etc.)
- Include an invitation to the parent–student orientation and a respectful and firm reminder that their presence, or that of another adult in the family's network of caregivers, was required if the child was to be accepted into the program—no adult, no enrollment
- Thank the parent for taking the time to talk and always restate in closing, "I look forward to meeting you at the orientation"

I emphasized with SGLs that this was a conversation with a conscious intent to make the parent feel welcome, comfortable, and respected as the child's caregiver.

On occasion, we would encounter a parent who gave a response such as, "I just signed that form because he asked me to. I didn't have time to read it, and it's okay with me if he comes." In these cases we would ask whether this was good time to describe the program and our goals. If the answer was positive, the conversation posed questions of this sort:

> Mrs. Jones, I'm sorry, what grade is Joey in? And which math class? How do you think he's doing in the class?
>
> Mrs. Jones, it's okay that he's not doing well in that class; that's part of the work that we will do. What class is he doing well in?
>
> If you don't mind my asking, why do you think he's doing better in that class than in math and science?
>
> Is there anything you could share with me that would help us work with Joey?
>
> What do you think we need to do to make sure Joey has a positive experience?

Such questions usually increased interest and created a willingness to at least come to the orientation. As the program became established and more well known, we used a similar approach with parents who initiated contact with us. We did not have a single occasion when a child who wanted to attend the program could not because a biological parent, or an adult member of the family network, failed to attend the orientation.

The student application process and the initial telephone conversations with parents to confirm their consent and participation in the parent–student orientation were key tasks of the first phase of establishing a relationship. Through this relationship we received parental endorsement to lay the foundation for a relationship between the student and the program staff.

We were very sure that the students did not necessarily have to be willing to attend—simply that they would be able to attend. Unlike one program director who said, "I look for effort and that get-up-and-go attitude," we looked for *potential* and *adult reinforcement*. With student potential and adult reinforcement, it was possible to nurture apparently uninterested, apathetic underachievers so that they blossomed into confident students at school, just as they were quite competent in other spheres of their lives.

Credibility in the eyes of parents and caregivers, and their explicit willingness to partner with us, made our work possible. An axiom of our work was: If we have not had a positive face-to-face conversation or a successful telephone call with the parent, we do not call with bad news. The first contact had to be a positive one; otherwise, it was very difficult to establish trust and mutual support with parents and family members.

The Parent–Student Orientation

The next opportunity to develop a relationship with parents was at the parent–student orientation. The explicit task was to share with them the intent of the program. The implicit intent was to make parents comfortable with us and earn their support. My opening remarks acknowledged returning students and parents:

> This is Mrs. C's daughter's second year in the program; she's doing quite well in geometry. Mrs. S's son was among our first graduates and helped us develop our track record of effectiveness. He now attends Morehouse University, where he is doing fine and, I hear, having a great time. We have many success stories, and we know that your children will be among our future success stories. We want to create a triangle around your child that consists of you, the program, and the school. With this kind of support, your child cannot fail. We welcome your children, and we welcome you.

When asked about their experience of the orientation, parents wrote down these comments:

> Very open and friendly. Very informative, direct, and to the point. The game we played broke the ice, and I enjoyed meeting new people.

> What I enjoyed about the meeting was the team effort of the staff and the parent participation.

> [I enjoyed] the goal-setting exercise along with complete explanations and applications.

> As a parent, you made me feel comfortable with the other parents. You talked clearly, and I could understand what your program is achieving for my children.

> [I liked] the openness of the meeting—talking with other parents about the similar or same problem with the kids.

The parent–student orientation was considered a success when parents reported that they felt welcome, comfortable, and supported, and they valued the opportunity to connect with other parents and our staff.

Telephone Calls to Parents

Relationship building was woven into the program's organizational structure for communication with caregivers. A good-news call and a positive first
encounter *always* preceded a bad-news call. In order to achieve this goal, we
paid special attention to the initial telephone call and made attendance at
the parent–student orientation mandatory. We rarely had a child act up before
or during the orientation, and of course we said nothing but good things about
them in the preprogram call. This meant that when, and if, we had to call
home with bad news, it was in the context of a mutually supportive relationship with an adult in the child's life that was already in motion.

Good-news calls: Weekly touching base- calls. Study group leaders were expected to make check-in calls to each parent every Friday. The SGLs got the
job done, and parents came to expect those calls, in which they got a snap-
shot of the week and usually heard good news about their child. One parent
said:

> I actually looked forward to that call, the message the tutor (SGL)
> left, because I started using it for my how-was-your-week conversa-
> tion. Or I would just say, "Your tutor called and said you were
> working hard and doing better." When I saw how good this made my
> child feel, it made me appreciate them taking the time to do that. It
> was a nice touch, because it seemed like they bent over backwards to
> keep in touch with you and keep you informed.

Another shared:

> They will take time to talk with you about your child and answer
> questions you have. I have learned a lot from those young people,
> and I appreciate what they do for my child.

This investment in regular communication was our method to build relationships with parents continuously and lay the foundation for successful conversations in more difficult situations.

Bad-news calls: Step 2 in the Series of Consequences. Our disciplinary policy
required a telephone call the second time a student violated a rule of the
program. This call was non-negotiable and was always made, even for seemingly trivial events. One hot afternoon, I had to make a couple of calls. I
knew that I had to hold the line on the little things if the big things were
going to stay in place: First one student comes with no pencil, and then others

start doing the same thing. Next, they come with no books and no home-work, and then they only want to do homework, if they remember to bring it. Then attendance becomes haphazard. Maintaining the standards was es-sential if we were going to be effective, so I made the calls and I made sure that the SGLs made calls.

Usually, one or two phone calls home were excellent memory boosters for our students. We had to endure the self-righteousness of students when they came and waved their pencils, displayed their books, and said, "You don't have to call my house today." Parents appreciated the calls, even if students did not. They expressed appreciation for Project Interface's imme-diate attempts to address any problems with their children (University of California, 1989a). One mother said:

> I don't like hearing about problems when they have been going on and on and on for a long time. I want to hear about it *early*, and I always did from Project Interface.

Another said:

> My child was failing math, and I did not hear about it until the report card came home. It was too late then. He was already back in general math before I heard about it. That's why I ended up bringing him here. And since he's been coming, I hear from somebody when something is not right. That means I can jump on it and take care of it.

The Monthly Feedback Report

The monthly feedback report was done on the last Friday of each month, and it was mailed home. It included the same areas that were acknowledged in the monthly achievement ceremony: attendance, effort, academic achieve-ment (as measured by scores on the weekly quizzes), and citizenship. There was also a space for comments by the SGL and a standing invitation to re-spond and to visit the program.

Growth and Maintenance of Communication

The SGLs interacted with parents on a daily basis. They would meet them in the parking lot, send notes home, and sit down to talk with them after the program. I remember one parent who was experiencing the transition of a child to junior high school and puberty for the first time. Her child's SGL reassured her, counseled her, and worked out mutually supportive agreements so that the child could not divide and conquer them. SGLs grew in self-confidence as they saw parents respond to them, and parents came to appreciate and respect them as well. Parents and caregivers shared with us the following comments regarding their interactions with program staff:

> The teachers [SGLs] are very direct and confident. This gives me a great sense of trust for my child.

> What is helpful to me is speaking with the tutors about the kids' weak and strong points. Also the tips on how to help them.

> The communication between the tutors and the parents and the communication with the parents helped me with ideas to help my kids.

> The personal meetings with the tutor of my child are really helpful—her warmth, caring, concern, and enthusiasm in tutoring really make me feel good. I know my daughter is going to blossom.

Parents perceived Project Interface as reaching out to involve them through letters, telephone calls, progress reports, monthly meetings, and field trips. All the parents reported feeling welcomed and comfortable at Project Interface, and they felt their confidence was justified as they began to witness the impact the program had on their children.

Parents reported positive changes in their children as a result of their participation in Project Interface, citing "improved grades"; "improved study habits and attitude"; "improved self-confidence in their ability to learn and achieve in school"; and "becom[ing] more focused on going to college" (University of California, 1989a, pp. 66, 67). Parents experienced their relationship with Project Interface as a collaborative effort between the program and the home. Project Interface's choices to use a positive and continuous communication style and to value family participation led to a partnership in which both parents and PI felt ownership of contributions to children's success.

PHASE 2: PARENT CONTRACT, SECURING PARENTAL SUPPORT AT HOME

We were thrilled when parents turned out en masse for our programs and events, especially the annual awards banquet. However, parental support and reinforcement at home were their most important forms of participation. I told my staff not to be overly concerned if we did not see a parent on a regular basis as long as the child was progressing and the parent responded when we called, especially for a conference or in step 2 in the Series of Consequences. I asked SGLs:

> Which would you rather have: a parent who attends all the events (even the nonmandatory ones), is always around the site, and has a child who is not achieving or participating, OR a parent whom you do not see on a regular basis but whose child is engaged, working hard, and making steady progress? Both types exist, and we have seen both types, haven't we?

I personally preferred the latter, because it meant that something must be going on at home. My philosophy was: If the child responds to me as he would if his caregiver were present, usually—not always—that means that we will get effort, cooperation, and progress.

The parent contract in Appendix Figure B.2 shows the specific requests we made of parents. Parents were required to monitor students' study time, provide encouragement, participate in Project Interface events, and be responsible for their children's adherence to Project Interface rules for students. We reviewed each of these requests with parents at the orientation and allowed time for questions, discussion, and comments. The contract served as a formal, outward symbol of parental endorsement and their decision to confer their authority on us as well as our acceptance as a member of their extended family system or network.

When conferences that included problem-solving sessions with parents and students were necessary, the relationship that began with families through our communications system expanded to another level. Formal parent conferences were usually held for two reasons: because of lack of effort or because of misbehavior. See Chapter 7 for discussion of conferences as part of the Series of Consequences and additional examples of program interaction with family members. Parent conferences at Project Interface had these characteristics:

- They were based on an existing foundation of positive outreach and intentional relationship building.
- They focused on the student's effort and potential for achievement.
- They were accompanied by regular positive communication with families:
  - Weekly touching-base calls
  - Monthly feedback reports
  - Parental participation in step 2 of the Series of Consequences for misbehavior
  - Informal, impromptu, and unstructured conversations with adult caregivers

- They were solution-oriented and required action of
  - The student
  - The caregiver
  - The program
- They held all parties accountable to one another.
- They were followed by monitoring of behavior and progress by the SGL, the caregiver, and the program director.

The conferences were typically held at Project Interface, though we were willing to make home visits when appropriate. Some of my most memorable conferences were held in students' living rooms or sitting around the dining table with parents and the student.

Effort Conferences

Our conferences on effort were a result of one or more occurrences:

- Students grew frustrated, got angry, and wanted to quit the program.
- Students' work habits were not improving.
- Students frequently did not believe that we would follow through on statements about working hard, bringing their materials, calling home, or asking parents to visit us on-site.

These conferences were called early in the school year, when it was clear that a student was not settling in and focusing on the work. Our students were bright and frequently unaccustomed to academic challenges. Sometimes they would refuse to sincerely try as a defense mechanism against failure. Students who required effort conferences were not, as a rule, disruptive, disrespectful, or in need of a review of the rules. They might display winning ways and personality, and they were frequently well liked by teachers at school and by study group leaders. Despite these qualities, their work, engagement, and achievement did not reflect their potential or, often, even their present skill level. I challenged students about their level of effort. I'd say, "Okay now, be honest with me—straight. If I asked you, on a scale of 1 to 10, how frequently you *really* tried in school, where would you say you would fall?" Frequently, students would give me that "you really wanna know?" look and say, "I'd rather not say."

The following actions indicated a lack of student effort.

- They consistently "forgot" materials and books.
- They goofed off in the study group.
- They turned in sloppy and incomplete work.

- They were frequently tardy.
- They earned report card grades at school that did not reflect their potential.
- They carried notebooks that had homework out of sequence and/or had no dates, or headings, subject-matter titles on the pages.
- They folded work into minute squares or arcane shapes and carried it in pockets or purses, not in the notebook.
- They frequently described schoolwork as boring, uninteresting, or too easy and silly.
- They often said that the homework didn't relate to anything real, so why bother.
- They often complained that their work was not really read or that they got little or no feedback on it.
- They employed charm and personality to deflect adult commentary on the issue.

We shared our observations with parents and students and worked through problem-solving sessions during conferences.

A Home Visit Establishes a Relationship with a Mother and Her Son

A visit to a student's home for a parent conference was the exception, not the rule. When one occurred, it was usually prompted by significant misbehavior by the student. One day, the students were in the small fellowship hall, the first church Allen Temple built. It was hot, and it was the end of a long day. Students were restless, and I finally threw the gauntlet down: "I will take the next person who starts up home." Of course, the next student was Reginald Cotton, one of my favorites, who was bright, charming, and used to working as little as possible. He simply thought that the rules did not apply to him and that he could get away with something that another student couldn't. In fact, students were watching to see whether or not Reginald left with me.

After I called and asked his mother whether I could bring him home so that we could talk a bit, off we went. On the way there, I had the surprise of the school year: Reginald pleaded with me not to tell his mother what he had done—he would get into serious trouble and even lose his privilege of going to the 8th-grade prom. He was almost in tears. I saw an entirely different young man from the cocky, self-assured, trash-talking, occasionally defiant student I was accustomed to. I told him that it was not something I wanted to do, or enjoyed, and that, in fact, I wanted to go home, too, but he knew I could not let him get away with what he had done and the rules applied to everyone—even him.

We arrived, and Mrs. Cotton, Reginald, and I spent the next 2 hours talking in the living room. We talked about the specific incident that prompted the meeting, about Reginald's flippant behavior and attitude, and about the fact that he was not working up to his potential. His mother put some hard questions to him, and we got around to talking about his dreams and plans.

He wanted to go to the University of the Pacific, and he wanted a football scholarship. We talked about what that would require. We talked about potential and about making his dreams real. By the time his father got home, we were finishing up; Mrs. Cotton and I had bonded, and Reginald was still going to the prom. She thanked me for taking time to come and talk with her; she promised a change in Reginald's behavior.

The Cottons became stalwart supporters—so much so that Mr. Cotton served as a chaperone for our student dances at the East Oakland Youth Development Center. He was a well-built former football player, and all he had to do was stand there. He would stay until the last child was gone and then take Reginald home with him. The Cottons enrolled Reginald's younger brother in the program after Reginald had moved on to high school. When he graduated from high school, Reginald did enroll in and play football at the University of the Pacific.

The episode had an impact at Project Interface as well. I did not have to take another student home, and students responded when I asked for order. When I overheard a student telling another one, "Dr. Bouie don't play," I knew I had gotten my message across that I was willing to keep my word, even when it inconvenienced me. I believed in reinforcement from families, and I knew it could make a difference if a positive relationship had been established between the program and the home.

The Role of Extended Family Members in Conferences

Many of my students regularly slept and ate at two, and sometimes three or four, different houses. They would stay over with older siblings, aunts, cousins, grandparents, and even close friends of their mother or another adult in the extended family. These extended family members were often available when the biological parent was absent, and frequently they had more influence with students, and ability to hold them accountable, than the biological parent. Part of our success in working with students and families came from our decision to involve extended family members as well as parents in conferences.

My beliefs about the value of working with extended family members were influenced and reinforced by the experiences of a friend and colleague who was a teacher. She called me one day very upset about an incident that had happened with one of her students. An 8th-grade student had returned to school after a suspension with her aunt; they were told that the child could not return to school because her mother had not come with her. My friend was actually embarrassed because she knew that not only had a family member been rebuffed; the aunt was the mother's *older* sister, meaning that she had significant influence not only in the child's life but also in the mother's.

In fact, the message the family was sending the school was that the suspension was taken *very* seriously because a senior member of the family was coming to represent the family. My colleague knew schools that operated under legal guidelines that required them to work only with biological parents, but she said:

> Many of our children had adults other than biological parents who shared or assumed responsibility for raising them. If I don't work with them, whom am I going to work with? What I do is get to know the families, and they know me. I get written permission from parents to talk to and work with other adults in the family. When I call, they talk with me and help me out. If I fail to acknowledge that relationship, I am telling the child that, as far as I am concerned, the role that this aunt plays in his or her life does not matter, regardless of its significance to the child. I can actually end up undermining the aunt's credibility and authority; the child concludes, "If the school doesn't listen to you, why should I?" Then, too, there is embarrassing an elder in the family—especially when she's with her niece—that lady is probably mother to both of them—her younger sister and her niece! This job is too hard for me to turn away a caring aunt who is willing to help me work with one of my 8th-grade girls—especially an elder!

I took my friend's message to heart. Over the years, with the consent of the biological parent, I worked with countless aunts, grandparents, and older siblings. My policy became: If adults feed the student, and the child sleeps at their homes, they *are* assuming parental responsibilities, and I will work with them.

An Effort Conference with an Aunt

I first met Mrs. Loughton when she came to enroll Kenneth in the program; she seemed nervous and somewhat apprehensive. "I'd like to enroll Kenneth in this program." I said, "Let's talk about it—is there a problem or something? You seem nervous." She responded, "Well, I'm not his mother, I'm his aunt." I told her, "That's not a problem at all. It doesn't matter who brings the child as long they are responsible for him and have legal custody or parental permission." She visibly relaxed and she breathed a sigh of relief.

Kenneth attended Project Interface for 4 years; I never met his mother. Neither he nor Mrs. Loughton volunteered any information about her, and I did not ask. An SGL asked about his mother. I said:

> I really don't know; they haven't volunteered it, and I haven't asked. You know, what we do here is kids. We don't do adults, and we don't do parents. We do kids, and we do it very well. All we need is one caring adult in the child's life who will help us hold that child accountable for doing his best in school. The rest is really none of our business. We couldn't help his mother; even if we knew her situation, we could do nothing whatsoever about it. Nothing. So, let's stick to the knitting; we *can* work with Kenneth and his aunt, and make sure we help Mrs. Loughton—and ourselves for that matter—by making sure Kenneth starts to work at his potential, and that is what we are going to do.

As the year progressed, I learned a great deal that was pertinent to our work. Kenneth was a delightful young person—bright, charming, and capable. Unfortunately, I also learned that he was one of the laziest children I had ever seen and was a master at using his bright smile and engaging personality to get out of work and anything else he did not want to do. Kenneth's primary problem was not that he did not understand his schoolwork; he simply did not want, or intend, to do it.

I talked with Kenneth and attempted to use *my* charming and engaging personality to cajole and encourage him into putting forth even a modicum of effort. I was unsuccessful. I soon saw that Kenneth was attempting to manipulate me just as he did many adults. When I said, "Kenneth, you know, I think it's time to involve your aunt in our conversations," he protested and immediately promised to work harder than he ever had in his life, but by this time, I no longer believed him. I called Mrs. Loughton to ask her to come for an effort conference about Kenneth.

Mrs. Loughton came, and she, Kenneth, his math SGL, and I all sat down and reviewed the situation. The SGL echoed my assessment that the main problem here was disengagement and lack of effort—Kenneth simply did not work. Kenneth looked at all of us. He turned his big brown eyes on Mrs. Loughton, who calmly said:

> I am not having it. I just am not having it. I strongly suggest that you get busy, and get busy in a hurry. Kenneth, that is why I brought you here—I know you are smart, and you are just not trying. That is why you are here.

Kenneth was shocked. He looked at her and then at me; the look he gave me was none too pleasant. I just shrugged and said that he was too bright and had too much potential to be in the 7th grade and not working to get into pre-algebra next year. I just could not see that. We concluded the conference with a "what I need to do differently" list by Kenneth that stated the ways in which he would increase his effort and improve his behavior.

From that day on, we saw a change in Kenneth's behavior. He started to come prepared to work and actually did his work. He stopped borrowing my pencils and paper because he had his own. He stopped trying to manipulate adults, and he actually worked with the SGLs. He eventually enrolled at the University of California at Berkeley, and Mrs. Loughton told me he wanted to teach. To this day, I do not know his mother's situation. Mrs. Loughton, his SGLs, and I did know one another and worked with one another.

My experience with Mrs. Loughton and Kenneth confirmed my friend's belief about working with caregivers who are not the biological parents. I saw that it was sometimes more effective to talk with a caregiver than the biological parent. Mrs. Loughton provided a home, and though neither biological parent was present, Kenneth had everything he needed to succeed. Mrs. Loughton assumed parental responsibility for Kenneth; she was an integral member of his network, and—most importantly, from my vantage point—Kenneth listened to her and loved her. And she could, and would, hold him accountable for his actions. That was the commitment we needed from a student's family member for a successful relationship and to ensure student success.

PHASE 3: ON-SITE PARTICIPATION
BY PARENTS AND FAMILY

Sometimes a conference was the only on-site involvement that a parent or family member had after the parent–student orientation. However, as parents and family members became more involved and saw the progress that their children were making, they often looked for additional ways to contribute, and many spent more time at Project Interface.

The involvement and contributions of parents and other caregivers supported staff and students alike. Staff felt affirmed and supported as they witnessed parents and caregivers contributing their time and energy to help do the work at the program. When students saw busy, and often tired, parents and caregivers working alongside the staff, it was clear to them that the program and their caregivers formed a team and that students were the focus of this work and care.

On several occasions, we overheard parents observing classes saying, "I'm just looking around," or "I'm paying a little visit," or "I just thought I would stop in to see how things are going." Parents frequently telephoned Project Interface either to speak with their children, inquire whether their children had arrived, or inform staff that their children would be arriving late or leaving early (University of California, 1989a).

Initially, we would simply call individual parents and ask them to help us with a specific task. As the program evolved, we became more effective at organizing their involvement. At the beginning of academic year 1988–1989, parents were given a schedule of meetings, which was followed by reminder letters and follow-up phone calls before each meeting. During the orientation, a volunteer information form was among the materials distributed. Parents were asked to indicate their preferences. We collected these forms and organized the responses so that we could contact the individuals for specific activities.

On other occasions, we simply called parents and asked them whether or not they would be available to help us with a task or activity. Getting the project newsletter out was always a chore, and we called parents to help us bundle newsletters and get them ready for mailing. Caregivers were involved in a variety of tasks, which included the following:

- Preparing the project newsletter for printing and mailing (Parents formed crews to label and organize the newsletters for bulk mailing.)
- Chaperoning students on field trips and project outings (I rarely participated in field trips because we always had parents to accompany our staff and students.)
- Providing transportation to the computer laboratory for students participating in our off-site computer program at Alameda College (Alameda College opened its computer laboratory to us on weekends. Parents provided transportation for all students who attended. Each Saturday, parents would arrive at Project Interface to shepherd students to the college; another set would arrive at the college to return them to Allen Temple.)
- Preparing refreshments for project programs
- Securing tables and contributions for the annual awards banquet (Parents asked employers, friends, and organizations to which they belonged to support the event.)
- Attending annual programs and ensuring that their children and family members attended
- Sitting in on study groups and being a caring presence around the program
- Securing donations and supplies for ongoing work (A parent supplied

us with coupons to local fast-food restaurants that SGLs could use as incentive awards.)

Although Project Interface did not have an active parental advisory board, there were several ways that parents participated in the program. They served on standing committees, helped with administrative tasks, served as role models and mentors, and attended the workshops and meetings held specifically for caregivers. They felt that the workshops were useful in helping them cope with the stress of raising adolescents, and they shared that they felt relieved when they heard that other parents had similar fears and concerns about their children's erratic and inconsistent moods, attitudes, and behavior. This served to normalize their experience and help them feel supported by one another and the program. Parents generally perceived their relationship with Project Interface as a collaborative effort between the program and the home (University of California, 1989a).

CHAPTER 10

Troubleshooting: Success and Sustainability

The plight of many minority programs centers around the fact the director is expected to wear too many hats without having the necessary staff support.
—J. Alfred Smith Sr., Senior Pastor, Allen Temple Baptist Church

EARLIER chapters have shown how we faced challenges within Project Interface, such as staff and student recruitment, curriculum development, and the role of parents. Projects face a number of challenges as they experience growth in the number of programs offered or in the size of existing programs, which can impact their effectiveness and sometimes their existence. Once a successful project has been created and implemented, organizations have to figure out how to maintain continued growth and stability. Many of the challenges that PI faced are typical of new project-based nonprofits. For Project Interface, success brought additional challenges of rapid growth and changes in the values and assumptions that were the foundation of previously effective policies and practices. This chapter addresses some of these challenges; examines solutions we attempted; and makes additional suggestions, offered in retrospect, that programs and organizations experiencing growth or transitions may wish to consider.

By 1988 Project Interface had become an established program whose achievements were recognized locally, statewide, and nationally. It had received numerous awards and recognition by significant organizations, including the following:

- The lieutenant governor of California's California Works Initiative
- Inclusion in *Breaking the Barriers: Helping Female and Minority Students Succeed in Mathematics and Science* (Clewell, Anderson, & Thorpe, 1992)
- Inclusion in *Blacks, Science, and American Education* (Pearson & Bechtel, 1989)

- The University of California Task Force on Minority Student Recruitment and Retention (University of California, 1989b)
- The San Francisco Foundation's Koshland Program Award for Outstanding Community Service

Project Interface also received awards and recognition from a number of local civic and professional organizations. The success of the original program propelled Project Interface toward continued growth.

By 1990 Project Interface was the nucleus around which a new organization, Interface Institute, was formed. In addition to Project Interface, the new organization housed four other programs:

Project Primer
The College Prep Study Group
The Mentoring Project
The Science Enrichment Collaborative

These were programs that I had designed, received funding for, and established. The process of implementation for new programs to complement Project Interface brought with it new challenges.

INSUFFICIENT INFRASTRUCTURE

While Project Interface was successful in meeting and overcoming many challenges to its programmatic success, the rapid growth and transition from a solitary program to an organization that housed four additional programs, had double the number of staff and sites for recruitment or programs, and employed five new program directors as well as a full-time development director and business manager proved overly taxing for the existing infrastructure. It is important to recognize and prepare for these realities:

- The energy and values that drive the core program do not automatically transfer to new programs and staff.
- The core program has the benefit of a collective history, memory, and sense of mission that new programs and staff do not have.
- Oral history and informal induction are important elements because, along with formal training and orientation, they create ownership and continuity.

In 1989 Project Interface did not have these structural pieces:

- A formal personnel manual
- An orientation and training process for new managers and their staff that addressed basic protocol and transmitted the history, values, and practices of the core program
- A transition process with adequate support for the program director of Project Interface, now the organization's executive director

Everyone entering the organization needed an orientation like the SGLs in the core program received. Ideally at Project Interface, every new staff member would have participated in a 2-week intensive training program. If staff did not own the ethos, values, objectives, and standards of the core program, they could not transmit them to their own staff and, importantly, to their clients.

OVEREXTENDED LEADERSHIP

At Project Interface, the individual who should have trained, monitored, and coached the new managers to transfer the standards and values that made PI effective to new programs was also expected to do the following:

- Work with the individuals and organizations who partnered with Project Interface in the new programs
- Staff the board of directors
- Maintain relationships with parents and with the immediate and larger communities
- Oversee five program managers, a development officer, and a staff accountant
- Create and staff the steering committee for the new Science Enrichment Collaborative (SEC)
- Raise funds for each of the new programs as well as for the core program
- Oversee production of a personnel manual and accompanying materials for the new organization
- Represent the organization on citywide commissions and in interagency collaborations

"Anne, you're good, but *nobody* could have pulled that off," one observer flatly stated.

The following things should be kept in mind during growth and transitions:

- The board of directors and staff should be fully aware of the workload of senior staff leaders and its implications for the organization, because that individual or those individuals will do the bulk of the work, in addition to existing tasks.
- If new staff feel very dependent on the senior staff and need a great deal of hands-on coaching, senior staff will not be able to provide that level of staff support while also completing current and new growth-related activities.
- The choice among gradual growth, a significant focus on staff training, and acceptance of new offers from funders is a balancing act that may require a decision not to accept new funds or to begin a new program at a particular time.

In order for a full and smooth transition to occur, new programs and staff need a significant amount of investment in time from senior staff in the early stages.

FUND-RAISING ROLES

There are roles for senior staff and for board members in making successful fund-raising a reality. Staff can do the following:

- Communicate their needs, suggestions, and capacity to the board through meetings or one-on-one talks with board chairs and members
- Work together with the board on a fund-raising strategy
- Complete fund-raising activities to the extent that the tasks are accepted as part of their job
- Accept only those tasks that they perceive as realistically doable.

The Board can do the following:

- Understand enough about program needs and operations to understand the impact of fund-raising responsibilities on staff.
- Make a clear decision about the contribution requirements and roles of each member and of the board as a whole in terms of how it will support the organization financially.
- If fund-raising is a major task of the board, specify how funds will be raised. Some options include:
  - Require a contribution of a specific amount from each board member
  - Include making calls to potential funders as a board member responsibility

- Require board members to obtain support from their companies and organizations
- Establish an atmosphere of proactive fund-raising

If a model is used that requires staff to do a substantial amount of fund-raising, the following questions should be considered:

- Is there a need for a staff member specifically devoted to raising funds?
- Is there enough staff support in program and staff supervision to allow a director or associate director to spend a significant portion of his or her time on fund-raising?
- Who can maintain relationships adequately with funders and potential funders for the organization?

CHANGES IN BOARD LEADERSHIP AND DIRECTION

Changes in organizational leadership bring many challenges. Programs and organizations experiencing transitions on the board of directors may wish to reflect on these characteristics of changes in organizational leadership and their implications for staff and programs:

- Each board chair has a different style as well as different preferences and priorities. Each new leadership group will need to reestablish itself and its direction.
- When a progression of chairpersons who share backgrounds and perspectives ends and leadership with very different perspectives begins, changes will occur. Dramatic change in an organization can occur in a short period of time.
- Changes in the direction of leadership can come at the expense of senior staff and organizational traditions.
- Leadership transitions are particularly difficult if other organizational changes occur simultaneously.

THE LOSS OF SIGNIFICANT ADVOCATES AND PATRONS

The maintenance of supportive relationships in the community is an integral part of organizational structure. While it is not always possible to continue relationships that benefit the organization and programs, the following things can be kept in mind:

- If the program or organization inherits a high public profile because of its patrons, sponsors, and founders, awareness of the political realities that accompany this situation is essential.
- A rupture in this type of relationship can have dire repercussions for the organization and staff; powerful sponsors can close the same doors their influence opened.
- Supporters who initiated relationships and actively sought to be involved with the organization may withdraw when they realize a politically sensitive relationship has been ruptured.

FUNDING CYCLES AND RESTRICTIONS

A program that expands and grows will encounter changes in the priorities and policies of existing and new funders, and it will work with foundations and corporate donors with an array of guidelines and criteria. It is clearly easier to write a proposal for a single program or organization, so small programs like Project Interface and new organizations like Interface Institute had to pay close attention to changes in policy and preferences when working with funders. The following characteristics should be kept in mind:

- Often funders express interest in the program but cannot provide operating or general fund support.
- Funders who have been involved with the program might indicate interest in a new program but not in the existing program.
- Foundations frequently examine and change their areas of focus and funding priorities or the way in which they will fund applicants.
- Often donors with large amounts of money will require the collaboration of several organizations. This requires significant time to convene meetings and work through the roles and areas of responsibility participating organizations would assume. Staff need to be prepared for the time and effort required to collaborate.

At Project Interface, interest from funders in new programs related to PI was the initial catalyst for three of the four new programs. PI's strategy for growth included:

- New programs that complemented the work of Project Interface
- New sources of funding that covered percentages of existing full-time positions while providing funds for a new program

A corporate program officer shared with me:

> I know that you need operating funds and general money for Project
> Interface. But we don't fund that way for multiple years. Even though
> the program is working, we expect you to have other sources of
> support. If we were to continue to be involved, it would have to be a
> new component of an existing program or a new program.

For any organization there will be ongoing fund-raising dilemmas:

- How is funding acquired for the core program and full-time staff who
  are not directly involved with new programs?
- How fast *can* growth occur?
- How fast *should* growth occur?
- Are there times when it is appropriate to turn down funds?

Each organization will have to answer these and other questions in its growth
and sustainability plan and as new opportunities arise.

There are challenges at every level of a program or an organization. Most
staff and organizations can survive any one of the challenges mentioned here
and some can withstand two, but very few can survive three or more of these
challenges when they occur simultaneously. The relationships of these challenges to one another and to my involvement with Project Interface are presented in the Epilogue.

Epilogue

... and we will know more later.
—Curtis Smothers,
personal communication

T HE PATH we built for middle school children to achieve academic success at Project Interface used these building blocks:

- *High expectations.* High expectations and a firm belief in the children's capacity to master rigorous work, and in our ability to help them do so, were the basis for the program.
- *A highly structured program.* The structure and routines established and maintained safe, secure boundaries. Consistently high expectations and consistency in the implementation of rules, consequences, and rewards was an ongoing and shared responsibility among staff that replicated the patterns of adult–child interaction found in students' homes and communities.
- *Challenging curriculum content.* The curriculum content was based on standards set by the state department of education and the Oakland School District; it showed respect for students' desire for more challenging work and their capacity to achieve at high levels, while addressing gaps in prior learning to assure mastery of the present material.
- *Engaging instruction.* Study group leaders provided instruction that combined the use of creativity and an awareness of students' developmental needs in the design of learning experiences that required collaboration, support, and sharing of knowledge among students. Learning experiences also demonstrated the relevance of the current content to students' aspirations and future learning goals in high school and college.
- *A nurturing program environment.* A high level of nurture throughout the program structure and activities created a context that cultivated student strengths and interests, while incorporating rigor and requirements for discipline, participation, and success.

- *Parents as essential program partners.* Relationships with parents provided a crucial element of support for students that a program alone could not provide; parents would not let their children give up and provided ongoing encouragement at home.
- *Community support.* Relationships with community partners were especially beneficial to PI in the recruitment process for students and SGLs by providing a location for the program and through donations of time, money, and expertise.

Many of the changes in the initial program came about naturally as we learned and progressed to the next steps of Project Interface on a programmatic scale.

The success of Project Interface in combining values and effective methods to serve our children did not carry over to the expanded organization to the extent that it might have had we not had such rapid growth or if our growth had not occurred simultaneously with significant organizational challenges related to board leadership, funding, and community relations. The board of directors was making its own transition in leadership, perspective, and priorities. The fund-raising and community relations strategies were changing with the new organization, Interface Institute. Project Interface was no longer an autonomous program; its fate and survival, as well as my own, became inextricably linked to the fate of the new organization.

The existing infrastructure could not accommodate the rapid new growth that occurred in less than 2 years while maintaining the strength of our belief in the students' ability to learn and the methods that formed the core of success in Project Interface. New staff managers could not train their own staff when they themselves had not been fully trained and oriented to the work. Without sufficient training and orientation to the oral traditions and stories that surrounded Project Interface, new managers did what they knew; what they knew were the prevailing practices and assumptions about how to work with urban youth. An incident around student expectations illustrates this point:

> I sat in on a staff work session at one of the newly implemented programs and had an opportunity to review notebooks that SGLs had asked students to compile. The notebooks were full of sloppy work and misspelled words written hurriedly. The work, in my eyes was completely unacceptable, and students should have been asked to redo it. I asked what the students had been asked to do, because I knew the work that I saw was not the best the children could produce, even before entry to our program.
>
> When I asked the program director to help me understand why work of this quality was being accepted, he told me that they "did

not want to make the students uncomfortable by correcting them or to interfere with the students' creativity" and that they "wanted to keep the learning fun."

I sighed and felt responsible for not having trained him more fully in the knowledge gained through the success of high expectations in Project Interface so that he could have trained his staff to adequately support our students and expect them to do their best. This revealed another challenge of rapid growth.

The overextension of my role left me responsible for the needs of the entire organization and in an untenable position with my workload unacknowledged and conflicting expectations from staff, board, partners, and clients. The more successful I became, producing organizational growth and acquiring funds from significant institutions and foundations, the more responsibilities were added.

I tried one-on-one talks with board chairs and members, this is one area where I did not communicate my need for support adequately. Unfortunately, my success conveyed the message that I did not really need the board, which was not correct. My success in getting new funds seemed to relieve the board of responsibility and allow them to focus on being supportive and involved without having to raise funds.

A community member with an intimate knowledge of the program observed:

> It is unfortunate that in addition to being the director of Interface Institute Dr. Bouie had to do the impossible task of fund-raising. It was also frustrating for her because often persons who could have garnered funds from the institutions that they represented did not.

The absence of stronger, more consistent involvement from the board in fund-raising meant that each year I faced a choice: to either watch the program fold or to increase the budget. Notwithstanding my frustrations with the board related to fund-raising, the board was continually a positive and affirming presence, and that support allowed me a great deal of freedom. That, however, soon changed when an incoming board chair saw problems; most of them were centered on me. Too late for a smooth departure, I realized that a single senior staff member could not manage the internal work of the organization and also be the public face that raised funds, especially with other organizational challenges occurring at the same time.

I served with five board chairpersons at Project Interface; all except the last belonged to Allen Temple or NCCBPE. Staff approached the incoming chair, a corporate executive, and confirmed his worst suspicions: that the problem lay with my inability to manage and grow with the organization. I saw this scenario developing and felt the new chair's lack of support; in hindsight, submitting my resignation when the new board chair assumed the position might have been the best decision, because it was clear from the beginning that the relationship I had had with previous chairs was about to change. The loss of a mutually supportive working relationship with the board chair was particularly difficult because it was accompanied by a significant loss in another critical area: community support.

It was a political and social reality that being housed at a large, powerful urban institution was a distinct advantage for Project Interface. The church was renowned for religious and spiritual leadership; further, it boasted a large, multifaceted ministry in the surrounding community. The church was not only well known and respected by nearly every segment of the community across the spectrum of race, ethnicity, social class, and profession; the institution wielded significant influence across a broad spectrum beyond the immediate community as well. Many individuals supported Project Interface not only because they cared about the education of urban youth but also because of its positive association with a powerful institution. The loss of such a significant relationship had profound consequences that affected our organization and rippled across the entire community.

In the end, my departure was the result of a great deal of rapid growth and change without a process in place to build a broad senior staff leadership that received the same kind of development and nurture that the study group leaders at Project Interface had received in earlier years and of my disagreements with new board leadership as the Interface Institute became a place very different from the environment that I had worked to create in Project Interface.

It is my belief that the new leadership of Interface Institute succeeded in running a tutoring program and expanding the organization. However, the founding beliefs that placed the education of children in the traditional context of community and family as well as the acknowledgment of a tradition of excellence and high achievement in the community, which stressed high achievement while firmly supporting students and their families, gave way to a less stringent curriculum with homework as a regular activity.

Movement away from these core beliefs signaled the end of the original context in which the achievement by our students was fostered, nurtured, and eventually attained. The new program context resulted in lowered expectations for student achievement and a decreased emphasis on rigorous training for study group leaders to fully prepare them to meet the demands of their role in the program. The new context also resulted in the perception of parents and community as the sources of problems rather than a crucial element in the solution to problems.

The founding beliefs in the capacity of PI students to achieve and in the capacity of their parents to support them are still relevant years after the project began. An episode with the same unruly group of girls mentioned in the Prologue, whom I worked with in Washington, D.C., in 2003, gives me hope; it is an interaction that demonstrated increased involvement in their academic work. After phone conversations with parents of most of the girls, I had begun to see positive changes in their behavior. Every Monday they were required to write an essay. Every Wednesday I returned the essay with feedback in red and suggestions for the next rewrite, which was to be done at home. Essays improved as the weeks went by. One week I was absent, and the substitute read and graded their papers. One of the girls looked at the unmarked papers without comments and said, "Ooh, she didn't even read our papers." Though I showed no reaction and made no comment, I knew that we were making progress. On one hand, it is frightening to think that the engagement and academic achievement of students can depend almost entirely on the context and environment in which they learn and are taught. On the other hand, it is heartening because so much that is needed to create environments where children thrive and parents and the surrounding community are allies, not adversaries, is within our control.

I have presented the story of PI not to promote its exact replication but to suggest that its core strategies, premises, and areas of focus could help educators grappling with the same problems that policies such as No Child Left Behind (NCLB) attempt to address today. The requirements outlined by NCLB place an emphasis on academic standing and the use of data to design policy, recognition of the role of parents in education, and establishment of accountability at all levels of the educational system. The following paragraphs are not an endorsement of NCLB. They show three key aspects of this law that are important to note, as they are addressed by the work at Project Interface.

First, disaggregated data allowed us to understand where our students were when they entered the program. The pretests SGLs designed during the summer were based on what students should know upon entering a given grade. Student scores on the CTBS test told us how well they had met that standard. At the end of each year, student data were used as a key component of the program's evaluation, along with a qualitative survey conducted by an outsider.

These data also influenced program policy and program design. Student progress and evaluation results were used in the development and modification of the specific content and activities for each year of the program. The processes woven into Project Interface were based on the reality that our students were quite competent in a number of areas; that they were often highly respected in their homes, churches, and communities; but that they suffered from years of low expectations and failure in school. This meant we had to design program experiences that acknowledged their competence and potential while addressing their gaps in learning and skills. The policy became to eliminate the use of words such as *tutoring*, *homework program*, *remedial*, and *at-risk*. Instead, we talked about students' capacity to achieve, enrichment, and the relation of academic goals to their future aspirations and their understanding of what it took to be somebody. The *processes* involved in the work at Project Interface created relationships and experiences that intentionally nurtured students' hope and provided our hope, along with that of their parents and the community, when theirs faltered.

The second relevant issue is an effort on the part of NCLB to acknowledge the essential role of parents in the educative process. As I shared earlier, Project Interface simply would not have existed without the endorsement and partnership of our parents and other caregivers. We worked to build authentic relationships with caregivers; we established credibility with them by acknowledging issues of importance to them and explaining how our program would address the issues. My more recent experiences with parents and caregivers reconfirm the power of developing relationships with parents and caregivers.

A third challenge that policy makers and practitioners struggle with today is the development of appropriate methods of accountability. Even though it was difficult for Project Interface to separate out other relevant factors affecting student achievement and we could not assume complete responsibility for the success or failure of our students, we had to be willing to adhere to some measure of accountability. Foundations, corporations, board members, and grandmothers all expected something from us: improved student achievement, and they asked for explanations when it was not forthcoming. Project Interface held high expectations of staff and students, maintained rigor in staff development and student learning experiences, and created an environment that fostered creativity, collaboration, and teamwork among the adults toward a common goal; this gave us the confidence to assume accountability for our students. We knew if we followed our procedures of working with students and using evaluations to improve, we would succeed.

We believed we could do it in spite of scarce resources and tight facilities, and we did. When SGLs would bemoan our lack of equipment or space, I would ask them to tell me which of two groups I would choose. One group worked in less than adequate facilities and was sometimes strapped for supplies and equipment. However, they were willing work hard together, and they believed that their students could and would achieve. The other group worked in state-of-the-art facilities with more equipment and space than they needed. However, they did not work together, and they believed that their students could not achieve high standards because poverty was the cause of their low test scores. SGLs would almost always say, "The first group." And I would say, "You're right. Money, equipment, and space are important, and I want all we can get. However, it is the set of beliefs and processes that infuse the equipment and the building and become the source of the program's effectiveness. Those are the important things—so get busy."

These processes and beliefs have been, are, and will be found in many different settings using an array of methods and techniques run by people as diverse as any group imaginable. I am grateful to have been a member of one of those sites.

Appendixes

Figure A.1. Partnership Creation Checklist

Building Relationships and Forming Partnerships

❑ Identify each partner's goals, ongoing work in the program's area of focus, and the areas in which each partner desires to expand.

❑ Facilitate discussions to create shared definitions of key words, phrases, goals, and objectives.

❑ Identify roles, responsibilities, rights, and privileges of each member.

❑ Identify a liaison to facilitate communication among all partners.

❑ Create, negotiate, and manage partnership agreements.

❑ Cultivate cooperation among partners.

❑ Arrange for informal conversations and contact among partnership members.

Figure A.2. Program Design Checklist

Program Design: Analysis of Problems, Opportunities, and Desired Outcomes

❑ Identify the program's client group(s) and goals and objectives.

❑ Identify the problems or concerns the program will address.

❑ Get input from an array of perspectives to define the problem.

❑ Conduct needs assessments that target the greatest needs.

❑ Analyze results of surveys from the needs assessment.

❑ Analyze feedback from volunteers with experience in other programs to build on successes and create improvements.

Figure A.3. Suggested Roles for Policy Makers and Practitioners

Suggested Roles for Policy Makers and Practitioners at Federal/State, Local, and Program Levels Related to Major Program Components

Establishing a Program: Developing a Framework for Goals and Creating Partnerships for a Strong Foundation

Federal- and State-Level Policy	City- and County-Level Policy	Program-Level Policy
• Ensure accessible, affordable, high-quality programs for school-age youth during nonschool times	• Clearly articulate the city or county goals and roles in supporting after-school programs, and articulate the ways in which these roles enhance current work by supporting existing leadership	• Use the creation of the mission statement as an opportunity to access, address, and include all stakeholders
• Ensure the inclusion of an array of participants in federally supported state and local service programs, including those with disabilities and special needs	• Municipal and county strategic plans for positive youth development should:	• Ensure that everyone in the organization can state the mission and explain how it influences their work

• Encourage meaningful partnership (including shared revenue and other resources) between community-based organizations and schools to provide a wide range of activities in nonschool hours	* Identify youth development as a broad public responsibility
	  * Support the primary role of family
	  * Include young people as partners in decision making
	  * Focus on fully preparing youth for meaningful participation in the economic, social, and political spheres of society
		• Identify and recruit potential board members who can give and get financial, human, and material resources that directly support the program mission

• Establish rewards and incentives for adherence to recognized quality standards	* Support the expansion of youth development opportunities provided by community-based organizations	• Design and implement a comprehensive training and orientation session for the board where program goals, objectives, and human and financial needs are identified and assigned to specific board members; include an accountability process for board member commitments
• Allow funding for renovation of facilities to adapt them for after-school programs and for transportation to and from programs; offer incentives for schools to use their buses	• Request that appropriate city departments and programs meet to explore ways to combine and leverage resources	• Review documents to be included in press or recruitment packets with specific target audiences in mind
• Support a national media campaign promoting the importance of youth service to help young people become confident about participating in community service, build public appreciation for their service, and promote youth as partners and resources.	• Provide resources to community youth development programs as an economically sound, front-end investment in youth that will eventually lower public expenditures for jails and prisons.	• Ensure that a structure exists to orient and coach potential volunteers and/or donors
	• Allocate funds to research program outcomes, distribute results widely, and support information networks to provide opportunities for professionals to connect research to practice	

149

(continued)

Figure A.3. (continued)

Suggested Roles for Policy Makers and Practitioners at Federal/State, Local, and Program Levels Related to Major Program Components

	Program Setup and Preparations	
Federal- and State-Level Policy	City- and County-Level Policy	Program-Level Policy
• Establish a resource guide or refer program planners to sources that provide information on academic standards and developmentally appropriate learning experiences for children at various age levels • Convene and build alliances with colleges of teacher education to place students in after-school programs with documented academic gains for students, particularly on local, state, and national criterion-referenced and standardized tests; additional measures could include improved school attendance or grades and success in challenging academic courses • Convene leadership of national organizations and civic, social, and professional societies to develop a coordinated approach to integrated services and support for after-school programs	• Delineate and maintain standards for program quality, particularly for those focusing on academic enrichment • Convene representatives from the corporate and small-business sectors, schools, community-based organizations, civic, social, and professional societies to create an integrated agenda to support after-school programs • Provide training and technical assistance to program staff; allow city staff to volunteer at programs; work with social services to involve elders with young people • Promote an adequate level of pay and benefits to workers to ensure high quality care	• Establish guidelines for recruitment procedures that address timeframes, application, and selection procedures • Make sure that the student recruitment pool is aligned with the program's mission • Research and develop clear staff criteria guidelines that are specific to your program • Secure adequate funds to allow sufficient time for professional development at the beginning of the year and on a weekly basis throughout the year to ensure that staff have the skills needed to accomplish the program's mission • Require curriculum content that meets state and/or national grade-level requirements • Require activities and learning experiences that are based on grade-level standards

150

Suggested Roles for Policy Makers and Practitioners at Federal/State, Local, and Program Levels Related to Major Program Components

	Working Directly with Children and Families in the Program	
Federal- and State-Level Policy	City- and County-Level Policy	Program-Level Policy
• Sponsor research that examines the characteristics of effective staff at after-school programs • Provide technical assistance that translates theory into practice so that research on best practices can be applied to produce positive program effects for students	• Provide incentives to assure that school-age care programs conform to the working hours of parents, including programs provided during the summer and other periods when schools are not in session • Provide incentives to private employers, including private not-for-profit employers, to increase their employees' access to quality and affordable after-school care • Provide funding for screening and training for paid staff and volunteers	• Clearly state program-specific definitions of key terms (e.g., parental involvement, on-site activities, parents as partners) and provide examples of associated behaviors and activities • Require a formal written procedure for the program rules and consequences, which establishes a specific point at which caregivers are to be notified and involved in addressing student behavior and effort • Request that staff provide data on student absences and disciplinary actions on a regular basis according to an agreed-upon schedule • Visit students and staff • Request data that demonstrate that staff members have a positive effect on student engagement, effort, and achievement, as defined by the program's mission • Provide opportunities for board members and other policy makers to listen to caregiver and parent ideas for program content and activities and use the data in program design and evaluation

151

Figure B.1. Student Contract

STUDENT CONTRACT

Student _____

Address _____ Phone _____

******

I, _____.

in the _____ grade understand that I will be permitted to attend

_____ as long as I do the following:

1. Attend all sessions with NO unexcused absences and/or tardies. If I am absent, I will bring a written excuse, and if I am tardy, I will enter the classroom quietly.

2. Be responsible for bringing materials (textbooks, homework, pens, pencils, paper, ruler, calculator, compass, protractor, etc.) for the subjects I will be taught.

3. Keep the sessions peaceful by respecting myself and all other persons in the room.

4. Raise my hand to be recognized for permission to speak.

5. Perform all tasks assigned to the best of my ability. Make corrections and practice on areas in which I am weak.

6. Be responsible for the program procedures as outlined in the Student Rulebook.

7. Complete my assignments, study at least 2 hours daily, and progress from grade

_____ to grade _____.

I have read the above contract and the Student Rulebook and pledge to uphold its contents as stated.

_____   _____

Student Signature   Date

Center for the Development of Schools and Communities

Figure B.2. Parent Contract

GUIDING PRINCIPLES: Explicit

PARENT CONTRACT

I, _____, parent of, _____,

am committed to doing whatever is necessary to insure that my child,

_____, puts forth maximum effort in school and Project

Interface to achieve as much as he/she is able to. Therefore, I pledge to do the

following:

1. Provide a quiet place where my child can study at least 2 hours daily.
2. Allow NO phone calls, television, music, or other interruptions during study time.
3. Ensure regular, consistent attendance at school and Project Interface.
4. Review my child's homework daily to see that it is complete and neatly done, and sign off each day on the weekly assignment sheet.
5. Attend 4 out of 6 parent meetings hosted by Project Interface.
6. Encourage and support my child to do his/her best in all subjects and at Project Interface so that he/she can and will make a progression from a level-2 work to level-1 work.
7. Participate in at least one ongoing fund-raising activity for Project Interface or serve on a regular basis on a standing committee.
8. Ensure my child's adherence to the Basic Student Rules and discipline procedure at Project Interface.
9. Make sure my child brings supplies DAILY (textbooks, homework, pens, pencils, paper, ruler, calculator, compass, protractor, etc.). A binder is needed to store project materials.
10. Be responsible for any and all acts my child does while at Project Interface.

I have read this parent contract and the Parent Handbook and pledge to uphold its contents and context as stated.

_____   _____

Parent Signature   Date

Center for the Development of Schools and Communities

Figure C.1. Summary of PI Quantitative Data

The Results at Project Interface: A Summary of Quantitative Data, 1982–1989

The CTBS provided three scores for interpretation and analysis:

- The *median score* converted the students' raw test scores to allow comparison of scores between years and across grades.
- The *grade equivalent score* reported the competency level at which students were functioning and the number of months' growth that had occurred during the school year; a minimum of 10 months' growth per year was expected.
- The *percentile score* reflected the students' standing in relation to a national norm group. A gain of 3 to 5 points was the minimum acceptable level as an indicator of increased competency.

For reporting purposes, Project Interface documented its own data in comparison with data from the three or four home schools from which the majority of its students came and with data from the district as a whole. Project Interface reported data in as user-friendly a fashion as possible. No complicated charts would befuddle parents or confound corporate sponsors. Plain English and straightforward graphs were used, with as few words as possible. We sacrificed specifics in most cases to a presentation of the bottom line.

Our data spanned 1982–1983 through 1989–1990. They reported our student performance on the CTBS for each grade we served; the total group at PI; three or four home schools ("home sites"); and the district as a whole. Our data also reported the number of students each year who matriculated to college preparatory classes, meaning they took pre-algebra as 8th graders, pre-algebra or preferably algebra as freshmen, and algebra or preferably geometry as sophomores.

1982–1983 Average Scores

The data were presented as summary data because all three grades made positive gains, and thus the average across grades was positive. In years where one grade level might not have done so well, we thought it prudent to present the scores for each grade as well as the summary data.

Median Score. PI 7th, 8th, and 9th graders averaged a stunning 53-point increase on their basic test scores, greater than at any home site or in the district as a whole.

Grade Equivalent. This score reports the number of months' growth students made during a school year. The average gain across the three grades for PI students was 17 months, almost 2 full years' growth. Only home site 3 and the district—both with 13 months' growth—exceeded the minimum 10 months' growth that should occur each year.

Percentile Rank. This score tells where a student, or group of students, stands in relation to the national norm. It is the most difficult score to move, since it is dependent on significant increases in students' raw scores. A minimum of 3 points' movement translates into significant activity. In 1982–1983, PI students made a 4-point increase, a gain surpassed by only one of the three home sites.

1983–1984 Average Scores

Median Score. PI students made an across-the-grade 15-point increase on their test score results; this average score obscures the 25-point increase made by 7th-grade students that academic year.

Grade Equivalent Score. PI students had an average 17-month growth during the school term. This average gain was boosted by a 21-month gain by 7th graders. Just one of three home sites (home site 2) and the total district made the 10-month minimum that year.

Percentile Rank. This difficult-to-move score skyrocketed with the help of a 24-point leap by the 7th graders, who entered at the 24th percentile and ended the year at the 48th percentile, just 2 points below the national norm.

1984–1985 Average Scores

A lengthy strike occurred in the Oakland Public Schools during the 1984–1985 academic term. Project Interface remained open and represented, in some cases, the only academic work students received for nearly a month.

Median Score. PI students scored an average of 9 points higher on the CTBS, while the home sites and the district—at best—made minimal gains.

Grade Equivalent Score. PI students achieved an average of 11 months' growth during the year, in spite of that strike. While 7th graders achieved just 6 months of growth, 8th graders achieved 10 months, and 9th graders 17 months—thus, the Project Interface average of 11 months.

Percentile Rank. The 9-point drop in the percentile standing of this year's 7th-grade class overshadowed the respectable 3 point gain by 8th graders and the 6-point increase by 9th graders. These scores average out to no increase in the percentile standing for the total group.

1985–1986 Average Scores

The major strike resolved, schools—and test scores—resumed a more predictable pattern. Note, also, that we included a fourth home site in the comparison; this school was reputed to be the best high school in the district, and our students outperformed that school overall.

Median Score. PI students increased their score on the CTBS by 14 points: 8 and 9 points by 7th-, 8th-, and 9th-grade students, respectively, averaging 10 points across all three grades.

Grade Equivalent Score. Gains of 13, 10, and 15 months for 7th-, 8th-, and 9th-grade students resulted in an average of 13 months' growth for program participants.

Percentile Rank. A 2-point drop by PI 8th graders dented solid gains made by 7th graders, who moved up 4 percentage points, and 9th graders, who made a 6-point gain. This resulted in an average 3-point increase for the project as a whole.

(*continued*)

Figure C.I. (continued)

1986–1987 Average Scores

The performance of our 7th-grade class was so dismal this academic year that we resorted to reporting it with the figures for each of the three grades so that our constituencies, particularly our board of directors and funders, would place their performance in context.

Grade 7. 1986–1987 was not a good year for any 7th graders, our students did quite poorly, showing a 2-point gain on their score for the year, a scant 2 months of growth, and a devastating 18-point drop in their percentile ranking. Individual students reported losses of 20, 30, and in one instance, 50 points on the test.

Grade 8. PI 8th-grade students made greater gains than those in the district as a whole and at all home schools except home site 1. PI 8th graders showed a 13-point increase on their test scores, a whopping 22 months of growth, and moved upward in their percentile ranking by 8 points.

Grade 9. Like the project's 8th graders, 9th-grade students made excellent gains, showing an 11-point increase on the median score, 22 months of growth, and a 10-point increase in their percentile rank.

Total Group. The excellent gains made by 8th and 9th graders were all but canceled by the 7th graders during the 1986–1987 academic year.

1987–1988 Average Scores

Data from school sites and the district as a whole were not reported for this academic year. The report accompanying the PI data states, "Traditionally, we have reported our students' performance in comparison with the schools they attend. This year, we have discontinued that practice and simply compare our students with themselves and the national norm. Data on individual schools, or the District as a whole, are available from the Research Officer of the Oakland Public Schools."

Grade 7. Seventh graders made no actual gains on their median score, resulting in a drop in their percentile ranking and a 3-month loss in their grade equivalency score.

Grade 8. Eighth graders made a 10-point increase in their median score, which translated into 11 months' growth for the year. Nonetheless, their percentile rank decreased 2 points; this was not statistically significant, but it still represented a decrease.

Grade 9. Ninth graders reported a mere 4-point increase on their median score, a scant 8 months of growth, and reported an actual decline of 4 points in their percentile rank.

Comparison with the National Norm. In spite of decreases in their percentile ranking, all three grades scored above the 50th percentile—8th graders at the 56th, and 9th graders at the 54th percentile.

This was obviously one of those years that nonprofits—whose mission speaks to academic achievement—do not like to report. It is the only year in which all three grades of students did not do well. Fortunately, by this time, the program had developed enough of a track record to be allowed an "off year." We did not like it; it meant that we had a great deal of reflecting and refining to do so that this year did not establish a pattern.

1988–1989 Average Scores

Project Interface resumed reporting data from school sites and the district as a whole for this academic year.

Grade 7. PI 7th graders showed a mere 6-point increase in their median score, which translated into just a 5-month gain during the year and a significant 11-point drop in their percentile ranking. They did not do as well as their peers at their home sites or in the district as a whole.

Grade 8. PI 8th graders performed admirably, making a 12-point increase in their median score, a solid 15 months of growth over the course of the school year, which translated into a very solid 6-point increase in their percentile standing.

Grade 9. PI 9th graders also did well. They showed a 10-point increase in their median score, a stunning 22 months of growth, and a 9-point increase in their percentile rank.

Total Group. The results of the total group indicate how a poor showing by one group can have an impact on the whole. The solid performances reported by 8th and 9th graders were essentially neutralized by the 7th graders that year. The increase of 9 points, a respectable 14 months of growth across the board, along with the solid increases in percentile rank reported by the 8th and 9th grades, reduced to a mere 1-point increase when the 3 grades were averaged.

1989–1990 Average Scores

Grade 7. PI 7th graders made a solid 12-point gain on the median score. This gain, however, was accompanied by just 8 months of growth over the course of the year and a percentile ranking that did not move.

Grade 8. PI 8th graders showed a 12-point increase on their median score, 13 months of growth during the school year, and a 6-point jump to the 59th percentile.

Grade 9. PI 9th graders, like their peers at their home schools, started out at the low end of the percentile scale. They showed a 15-point increase on their median score, a solid 14 months of growth over the year, and a very respectable 10-point increase in their percentile ranking.

Total Group. This year's total group score shows what happens when all three grades do well. The median score for the total group shows a 13-point increase; the growth for the group over the year was a solid 11 months, and the percentile increase was a respectable 5 points.

Figure C.2. Program Characteristics

The following chart, based on experiences at Project Interface, provides a broad overview of characteristics to consider in educational program design.

Program Characteristics

Program Characteristic	Examples of Effective Programming	Signs of Ineffective Programming
Expectations: Mission and Goals	• A clear mission statement exists. • An explicit program philosophy and ethos are present. • All staff can state the mission and goals.	• Staff cannot state the program's mission and goals. • Staff respond differently to queries about the program's mission and goals.
Expectations: Program's Perceptions of Students	• Students' and families' cultures are perceived as sources of strength, not pathology. • The program operates on a model that identifies and works with students and caregivers as partners to create mutually supportive and reinforcing relationships with one another to work together for the best interests of the children. • The deficit model is not present.	• Students are allowed to use excuses about circumstances as a reason for not working. • Staff state that environmental circumstances prohibit students from learning. • Staff state statistics about poverty and crime as the primary reason for student misbehavior and disengagement. • Staff cite lack of parental involvement as the primary explanation for student misbehavior and disengagement, and no relationships with caregivers have been established.
Structure: Staff Commitment to High Expectations for Students	• Diverse, well-trained staff have high expectations for student behavior and academic achievement. • Staff are invested in student achievement. • Staff motivate, encourage, and insist that students keep working to their potential. • All staff members communicate a consistent message, regardless of style and manner of teaching, job title, and subject-matter expertise.	• Staff do not push students to work hard. • The first draft of student work is accepted as a measure of a student's ability. • Work of any quality is accepted. • Staff state that circumstances beyond the students' control are the primary reason that students do not meet attendance, engagement, or achievement goals. • Staff state that parents are not assuming responsibility, but they have not attempted to develop mutually supportive working relationships with parents or caregivers.
Structure: Commitment to Strong Staff Development and Training in All Areas	• Ample time for staff training is provided to create a stable environment for staff and students. • Content, process, and cultural issues are addressed. • Training occurs before the program begins and is designed to create task-oriented relationships among staff, a sense of teamwork, and the ability to give and take constructive feedback well.	• Staff members receive training materials and are told to become familiar with them on their own. • Staff do not have the material and equipment needed to work with students effectively. • Staff do not have time allocated on a weekly basis for cooperative planning, lesson review, and coaching sessions.
Structure: Rules	• Clearly stated rules are implemented by all staff consistently in a firm, friendly, and fair manner. • Rules and consequences are thoroughly reviewed and explained with caregivers present, in the large assembly of students, and in small groups.	• The series of consequences is not consistently implemented by all staff, e.g., a student is sent to the director's office (step three) and no call is made to caregivers previously in step two. • Program rules are not consistently implemented by all staff. • A parent says that s/he was not aware of the student's misbehavior. • Effort calls and conferences do not occur.

Program Characteristic	Examples of Effective Programming	Signs of Ineffective Programming
Structure: Caregivers	• Caregivers are directly involved and endorse the program and its work. • Students' caregivers are essential to program effectiveness. • Caregivers work in positive and mutually supportive relationships with program staff to help students feel grounded and secure.	• Caregivers do not believe staff when they call home. • Staff see no changes in the behavior of students (with the exception of a small percentage of students that may truly be out of control). • Caregivers do not have informal casual conversations with staff while on site. • Student attrition is high and attendance is poor.
Structure: Evaluation	• Evaluation includes qualitative and quantitative data. • Program goals guide the use of evaluation data. • The purpose of collecting evaluation data is to assess program effectiveness. • Objectives are stated in measurable terms, and data help determine how well the program is serving its students. • Qualitative or hard data show that the program is having a positive effect on student engagement and achievement.	• The program relies solely on testimonials and feel-good stories. • The program's objectives are not stated in measurable terms. • There is no annual report or presentation of the year's work.
Content:	• Strong, standards-based academic components are designed to teach the skills and competencies that students need to develop. • Students use content from lessons to produce the work required. • Learning experiences are designed to address gaps in student learning, help students master current work, and prepare them for new learning. • The content is presented in ways that build on students' current interests, outlooks, and concerns.	• Staff use prepared material without adaptation to the setting and the children being served. • Staff give worksheets with "drill-and-kill" exercises to students. • Student receive graded work with little or no direct feedback or suggestions for improvement.
Pedagogy: An Indirect vs. a Direct Approach	• The program uses an indirect vs. a direct approach to student deficiencies and potential problems, acknowledging that students already know they are not doing well. (Just as there is a stigma to using free lunch tickets in the cafeteria, there is a stigma attached to needing tutoring and remedial help. Therefore, the most effective way to connect with students and increase the possibility that they will risk failure once again is to focus on their strengths, dreams, and possibilities.) • Staff pose appropriate challenges to students. • Staff show students how their accomplishments relate to their dreams for themselves (refer to the chart on Bloom's Taxonomy in Appendix G.1 for more specific suggestions).	• Assignments are too easy for students. • The work is dumbed down. • Assignments involve coloring and other activities that make no demands on students.

(continued)

Figure C.2. *(continued)*

Program Characteristic	Examples of Effective Programming	Signs of Ineffective Programming
Pedagogy: Learning Experiences	• Learning experiences blend staff-directed and student-directed activities. • Student interests are addressed in most learning experiences in most subjects. • Staff incorporate these interests into content and create student buy-in.	• Staff make no effort to personalize lessons to student interests. • Staff use packaged materials that are not reviewed and reworked.
Nurture: Students	• Staff pay explicit attention to social inequalities around race, ethnicity, gender, language, sexual orientation, and physical disabilities to help students develop positive coping skills and the ability to persevere in the face of obstacles and setbacks.	• Students say that the program staff are not fair or play favorites. • The program ignores or dismisses student complaints about unfair or prejudiced treatment. • Students tease and harass one another around these issues and adults do not censor their activities. • Students are not asked to assume responsibility for their contribution to bad situations. • Adults are not asked to assume responsibility for their actions and attitudes. • In situations of student–adult conflicts students are reprimanded and sent back into contested situations without assistance in efforts to solve the problem.
Nurture: Program Support	• All program components and activities are designed to intentionally reinforce and complement the program's core activities, mission, and goals. • Staff are able to explain how a given activity supports the program's mission and helps achieve programmatic goals.	• There are makeshift activities for children to fill time. • The program components do not fit together and reinforce one another. • Various components are not connected common objectives. • Activities are done in isolation from one another.
Nurture: Community Involvement	• Direct program support comes from a variety of sources, including volunteers, parents, and organizations.	• The program is isolated and does not have networks and relationships with surrounding and larger communities. • In-kind contributions are rare. • Volunteers do not return, or they do not get deeply involved in the program.

Figure D.1. SGL Training Outline

Trainers will work with Study Group Leaders to develop competency in the following skills:

Academic Content
Classroom Management
Task Analysis
Communication Skills
Parent Involvement
Discipline
Collegiality

Academic Content: Study Group Leaders will develop lessons that teach math and science effectively. An effort is made to integrate the two disciplines—teaching math by showing how it is used in science fields, and using math while learning scientific concepts.

Classroom Management: Study Group Leaders will develop systems for managing classroom materials and information.

Task Analysis: Study Group Leaders will develop the communication skills needed to work with school faculty, teachers, parents, each other, and the students they teach.

Parent Involvement: This is a very important part of our program. Parents are considered an integral part of making our programs successful. Study Group Leaders will demonstrate the ability to use different strategies of getting parent feedback and involvement in programs.

Discipline: Study Group Leaders will gain the ability to utilize disciplinary methods that are appropriate and effective.

Collegiality: Study Group Leaders will learn to work together and reflect on each other's work as a group.

Figure D.2. SGL Contract

STAFF CONTRACT

I have read the Project Interface Staff Handbook and understand its content and context thoroughly. Therefore, I pledge to uphold the following guidelines.

1. To respect myself, co-workers, students, parents, and anyone I come in contact with while at the project.
2. To be of professional manner at all times.
3. To use my teaching, mentoring, and advising ability in helping any student at any time.
4. To be at the work site on time and, if absent, to give an early notice.
5. To adhere to the dress code at all times.
6. To maintain a learning environment that is conducive to all involved.
7. To enact the discipline policy whenever needed.

I hereby pledge to uphold the contents of this contract and the Staff Handbook to the best of my ability.

_____   _____
Staff Signature   Date

Center for the Development of Schools and Communities

Figure D.3. SGL Observation Checklist

Checklist for Observing Study Group Leader (SGL)/Student Interaction

TEACHING SKILLS

1. Does the SGL keep all students working on the assigned task during the allotted time?
2. Does the SGL only call on students that he/she knows have the right answers?
3. Does the SGL give complete answers to all students' questions?
4. Does the SGL encourage all students to be academically competitive? Even those students who are behind the others in the group?
5. Does the SGL make sure the students understand the material? Does he/she present the material in different contexts to determine if the student has a thorough grasp of it?
6. Does the SGL compare students and/or their work?
7. Does the SGL ask the students questions that lead them to the answer rather than giving them the answer?

PREPARATION

1. Does the SGL explain activities and concepts clearly?
2. Does the SGL make sure that his/her students are prepared for the discussion each week?
3. Does the SGL state directions in a positive form? (For example, "Use the formula in this manner" instead of "Don't do it that way.")

CONSISTENCY

1. Does the SGL give each student the same number of opportunities to answer questions? Even if the student doesn't know the answer?
2. Does the SGL's pattern of response vary from one ethnic group to another?
3. Does the SGL consistently ask difficult questions of some students and easier questions of others?
4. Is the SGL arbitrary or consistent in disciplining each student?

CHARACTER

1. Is the SGL an instructor or an academic coach?
   a. Does he/she use supportive and inspiring language and praise each student on his/her accomplishments?
   b. Does the SGL have a personal stake in each student's success?
   c. Does the SGL push each student to complete the challenging tasks?
   d. Does the SGL take the time to explain the lesson plan's relevance to the student's life?
2. Is the SGL sincere when he/she interacts with each student? Does he/she sincerely express his/her interest in and love for each student?

GROUP WORK

1. Does the SGL monitor the group work process?
   a. Does the SGL set up the project explaining each student's role and purpose of the project?
   b. Does the SGL defer questions back to the group instead of always answering directly?
   c. Does the SGL make sure that no one dominates the discussion?
   d. Does the SGL make sure that the "low-achieving" students have an important role to play?
   e. Does the SGL stop the process when he/she sees it's not working and teach group work skills again?
2. Does the SGL monitor the students' work in the study group?
   a. Does the SGL make sure the students have all the resources they need and that they use them?
   b. Does the SGL have a plan for additional activities that are related to the students' needs if his/her students finish early?
   c. Does the SGL bring the activity to a timely conclusion?

Figure D.4. Water Properties Lesson

UNIT: Water   Cover Sheet
LESSON: Water Properties: Phases & Surface Tension
SCIENCE STRAND: Physical Science

I. OVERVIEW
    This lesson explores some of the physical and chemical properties of water in its three phases:
solid, liquid, and gas. Students will observe water in each of these three phases and perform simple
experiments challenging them to predict and measure its behavior. Students will also explore
surface tension and how it affects water behavior. The *Introduction* provides demonstrations and
discussion suggestions designed to spark the students' interest in water, including a role-playing
exercise where students act as water. The *In-class Activities* have students measuring and changing
water temperature, using different temperature scales, and forming and testing their own
hypotheses. The *Follow-up* section offers additional activities exploring phase-change properties,
surface tension, and the effects of chemical structure on behavior.

II. OBJECTIVES
    The discussion topics and activities provided are designed to increase student awareness and
respect for water; its composition, physical, and chemical properties; and how these properties affect
its behavior. Students will form and test their own hypotheses and use many data-collecting,
organizing, communicating, and interpretive skills as they discover for themselves the nature of water.

A. *PRINCIPLES*
    1. water has three phases
    2. water has unique chemical content and properties
    3. water's chemical content determines its properties and behaviors

B. *CONCEPTS*
    1. evaporation, condensation, precipitation
    2. phase change
    3. surface tension
    4. polarity
    5. freezing and boiling point
    6. chemical bond

C. *FACTS*
    1. there are three phases of water: solid, liquid, gas
    2. water is a compound composed of 2 parts hydrogen, 1 part oxygen
    3. water's freezing point = 0 degrees Celsius, 32 degrees Fahrenheit
    4. water's boiling point = 100 degrees Celsius, 212 degrees Fahrenheit
    5. Fahrenheit = Celsius × (9/5) + 32 degrees

D. *SKILLS AND COMPETENCIES*
    1. measuring
    2. collecting data
    3. organizing information
    4. graphing
    5. estimating
    6. following directions
    7. formulating hypotheses
    8. communicating

E. *VALUES AND ATTITUDES*
    1. respect for the importance of water: for sustaining life and its various functions in society
    2. appreciation for the complexity of water: its physical and chemical properties
    3. respect for water and the need for responsible use

UNIT: Water   Lesson Outline
LESSON: Water Properties: Phases & Surface Tension
SCIENCE STRAND: Physical Science

Suggested Agenda:
 Day 1: (I) Introduction, (II) In-Class Activities
 Day 2: (III) Follow-up, part A
 Day 3: (III) Follow-up, part B
 Day 4+: (III) Follow-up, part C

I. INTRODUCTION

A. *Mini-Lecture and/or Videotape:* The phases (solid, liquid, gas) and properties of water.

B. *Demonstration:* "The Three Phases of Water"—water will be heated from ice to liquid to vapor in a flask; the vapor will travel through a tube and recondense in another flask.

C. *Student Role Play:* Students hold hands and form the structure of water molecules in the solid, liquid, and vapor phases.

II. IN-CLASS ACTIVITIES

A. "Measuring Water Temperature":

 1. *Procedure:*
   a. prepare 4 water samples, each at a different temperature: boiling, tap, room temperature, and ice water
   b. measure the temperature of each water sample, using both Celsius and Fahrenheit thermometers
   c. record data on a data sheet
   d. perform unit conversions between the Celsius, Fahrenheit, and Kelvin temperature scales
   e. construct bar graphs of the data: water sample temperatures, different scales

 2. *Materials:*
   a. thermometers—Celsius and Fahrenheit
   b. ice, tap, and "boiling" water (use very hot tap or recently boiled water)
   c. containers to hold water: ice, boiling, and room temperature

 3. *Wrap Up:*
   Lab report, including procedure, observations, data, graphs, conclusions

B. "Changing Water Temperature":

 1. *Procedure:*
   a. prepare ice, tap, and "boiling" water
   b. measure the temperature of each water sample
   c. have students estimate the amount of ice water required to cool the boiling water to the tap water temperature
   d. add a specific amount of ice water to the boiling water
   e. have students record (on data sheets) the amount of ice water added and the change in temperature
   f. repeat steps (d) and (e) until the desired temperature is reached
   g. students graph the change in temperature vs. amount of ice water added

 2. *Materials:*
   (same as part A. "Measuring Water Temperature")

 3. *Wrap Up:*
   Lab Report, including: procedure, observations, data, graphs and conclusions.

(*continued*)

Figure D.4. (*continued*)

III. FOLLOW-UP

A. Boiling Point/Freezing Point

"Salt water vs. Tap water"—Students measure, record, and graph the differences between the boiling and freezing points of tap water and salt water.

B. Surface Tension:

1. "Water on a Penny"—How many drops of water can fit on a penny? Why?

   a. *Procedure:*
      1) estimate the number of water drops that will fit on a penny
      2) test your "hypothesis"—count the number of water drops the penny will hold
      3) record the data: penny surface (heads or tails), number of drops
      4) repeat for the other side of the penny—do you expect a difference? Why or why not?
      5) Optional: repeat procedure using the "red" and "green" drops of the following experiment: observe, record, graph, and discuss the results.

   b. *Wrap Up/Discussion:*
      1) Did the penny hold more or less water than you expected?
      2) What is the shape of the water on the penny? Why?
      3) How does "surface tension" and the "polarity" of water affect the shape?

   c. *Materials*
      1) pennies (one per group)
      2) eye droppers (one per group)
      3) water

2. "Red Drop/Green Drop"—Surface tension and soap.

   a. *Procedure*
      1) prepare droppers full of "red water" and "green water"
         "red water" = water + red food coloring
         "green water" = water + green food coloring + one drop of soap
      2) distribute sandwich bags and toothpicks
      3) allow students to "play" with red drops for 2–5 minutes (place drops on the bags, using the toothpicks to manipulate them)
      4) students record their observations of the red drops' behavior
      5) repeat steps 3 and 4 with the green drops

   b. *Wrap Up/Discussion:*
      1) Did you notice a difference in behavior between the red and green drops? What was it?
      2) How did the soap affect the behavior of the water drops?
      3) Discuss the terms: surface tension, polarity, hydrophilic, hydrophobic

   c. *Materials:*
      1) liquid dish soap
      2) red and green food coloring
      3) sandwich bag or sheet of wax paper (one per group)
      4) eye droppers (at least two)
      5) toothpicks (one or more per group)
      6) water

   d. *Resource:* "Science on a Shoestring"

3. "Pepper and Soap"—Demonstrate the hydrophobic nature of soap

    a. *Procedure:*
      1) float pepper on the surface of the water
      2) add one drop of soap to the water
      3) record observations (pepper will rapidly disperse)
      4) repeat (using already soapy water)

    b. *Wrap Up/Discussion:* Hydrophilic vs. Hydrophobic
      1) What happened to the pepper when the soap was added?
      2) Discuss the terms: hydrophobic, hydrophilic
      3) What happens on the second trial, when the second drop of soap is added?

    c. *Materials:*
      1) large bowl (or other container to hold water)
      2) ground pepper
      3) liquid dish soap
      4) water

4. Other Ideas

    a. *Density of Ice*—Most substances contract when cooled from the liquid to the solid phase. But not water! It is one of the few substances that *expands* when it is frozen. Consequently, the density decreases. This is very important because in cold conditions, ice forms and remains on the water surface, allowing life to exist underneath, in the ocean, lakes, and streams. Simple experiments can be conducted using ice, water, and salt, demonstrating the difference in density between water, ice, and salt water. Remember: *density = mass/volume.*

    b. *Water Composition*—The composition of water vapor can be discovered using a Hoffman apparatus (an electrolysis device). This device will separate the water into its component oxygen and hydrogen parts, then a flame test can be applied to prove the existence of the gases.

    c. *Standard of Measurement*—Water is such a common substance that it is used as a standard of measurement for many scales. The most commonly used are: gravity, pH, temperature (0–100 degrees Celsius), mass, heat energy (calories).

IV. RESOURCES

A. *Organizations:*
1. EBMUD (East Bay Municipal Utility District)
2. Levine-Fricke

B. *Books:*
1. *Earth: The Water Planet*; published by NSTA (National Science Teachers Assoc.), Washington, DC
2. *175 Science Experiments*; Brenda Walpole, Random House
3. *Science on a Shoestring*

C. *Curriculum, Educational Programs, Museums:*
1. Lawrence Livermore Labs "Lessons" programs
2. Lawrence Hall of Science—lists (by topic) of video and computer games

Figure E.I. Curriculum Design and Development

This chart contains a map of our curriculum design and development strategy along with suggestions and indicators for effective implementation.

CURRICULUM DESIGN AND DEVELOPMENT:
SUGGESTIONS AND INDICATORS GRID FOR EFFECTIVE IMPLEMENTATION

Component	Quality Standards Questions	Effective Implementation	
		Suggestions	Indicators
Content Standards and Grade-Level Proficiency Expectations	• Has the program identified the subject areas it will offer? • Have staff received training in the content standards of subjects the program offers? • Have staff received training in the continuum of grade-level proficiency expectations for the students that the program will serve? • Is training and/or technical assistance available for staff? • Are supporting materials (textbooks, workbooks, prepared programs, etc.) available for staff use along with the content and proficiency standards?	• Contact and develop partnerships with state, county, and/or local education offices for materials, training, and technical assistance. • Contact schools attended by students in the program and develop joint training workshops for program staff and teachers at the schools. • Assign two or three staff people to learn the material and become on-site resources for other staff.	• Each staff member has a copy of the state content standards and/or easy, on-site access to them. • Collaboration and cooperation with state and/or local agencies provides human and material resources to support staff learning. • Sufficient time is provided for staff orientation and training in the content and proficiency standards. • Staff can state and describe state content standards for the subjects covered by the program. • Staff can describe the grade-level proficiency standards students need to master. • Staff are assigned areas of specialization and responsibility, e.g., grade levels, content areas, skill sets, etc.

Effective Implementation

Component	Quality Standards Questions	Suggestions	Indicators
Planning Templates	Are templates available for staff use in curriculum planning and design and in the arrangement of content into yearly, semester, grading period, weekly, and/or daily formats? • Year-long templates provide an overview of content to be covered, broken into large segments. • Semester-long templates divide the year. • Grading-period templates outline content and skills to be covered during the period. • Weekly plans are detailed outlines of content and process to be used in teaching. • Daily plans show an activity-level plan for each day's work.	• Identify a model or approach that lends itself to informal educational settings (e.g., the Algebra Project, the FoxFire Project, the Professional Development Program, Project Seed, the Detroit Pre-College Engineering Program). • Design and/or secure planning templates for use by staff for the timeframes desired by the program (some learning experiences may not require long-term plans). • Secure training and coaching for staff so that they learn the role of all templates and how to use them to outline and design simple yet high-quality learning experiences that meet grade-level proficiency standards and contain appropriate subject-area content.	• Staff can describe the contents and use of any templates agreed upon by the program. • Staff can actually use the templates in their work, and a review indicates that they are using them correctly.
Design of Learning Experiences	• Do staff collaborate on and plan learning experiences in a regularly scheduled time period? • Are staff lesson plans reviewed by a supervisor, team leader, and/or a coach or trainer who supports program staff? • Do learning experiences state measurable objectives for student learning? • Do learning experiences include the proficiency standards? • Do learning experiences address gaps in student learning, mastery of current material, and introduction to new material? • Are learning experiences multidisciplinary when possible?	• Provide collaboration, review, and reflection time in the design of learning experiences using state standards, district grade-level proficiencies, and planning templates before the program year begins. • Provide a structured block of time each week for team planning and problem solving. • Provide coaching, training, and feedback for staff plans. • Provide opportunities for staff to share work with one another and provide one another with feedback and suggestions for improvement. • Provide staff with examples of learning experiences that include the desired skills.	• Collaborative staff planning is done weekly, is regularly scheduled, and staff adhere to the plans. • There is a checklist or criterion sheet that is used as a standard for lesson review that includes key points, e.g., includes appropriate content, proficiency standards, combines subjects, etc. • Lessons are reviewed by a staff supervisor and/or a coach or trainer who works with staff. • Learning experiences combine more than one subject and/or skill-building exercise, e.g., a science project that uses mathematics and requires a written report and an oral presentation.

(continued)

169

Figure E.1. (continued)

Component	Quality Standards Questions	Effective Implementation	
		Suggestions	Indicators
Relevance of Curriculum Content to Students' Subjective Experiences and Aspirations	• Do the learning experiences created by staff acknowledge and build on the daily lives and experiences of students? • Do the learning experiences acknowledge and include the contributions of women as well as religious, ethnic, racial, and cultural groups? • Does the curriculum address the aspirations and expectations of students and their caregivers? • Do the learning experiences include topics of concern to the adults in the immediate community? • Does the program access human and material resources from the community to include in its learning experiences and program activities?	• Acquaint staff with the community by inviting community representatives and parents to talk with staff. • Create processes and opportunities for staff to become familiar with the surrounding community. • If staff are familiar with the immediate community, use this knowledge to identify community resources that can support and inform learning experiences and program activities. • Invite parents, caregivers, family, and community members to share expertise related to subjects and activities offered by the program.	• Current events, local nuances, and student interests are built into site-based lessons and activities to capture and engage children's attention and interest. • Students are involved in choosing the content and planning the lessons. • Caregivers and family and community members are invited to the program on a consistent basis to support and enhance learning experiences. • Community resources that can enrich the curriculum have been identified and are used regularly.
Assessment of Student Competency	• Does the program have a process to pretest students that collects baseline data on their competency in the subjects that the program offers? • If using a prepared test, have staff been trained to administer and score it properly? • If staff are developing a pretest, have they been coached on its design and composition? • Are any of the program's partners involved in reviewing the pretest and providing feedback?	• Secure a prepared pretest and train staff to administer it. • If the program decides to create its own pretest, divide the staff into the appropriate subject-area groups and use the content standards and proficiency expectations to create a pretest. • Secure an external review of the pretest to assure quality and accuracy. • Provide staff with time to prepare, administer, and score pretests.	• Staff can use the proficiency standards to create a useable pretest for assessing students and/or access an instrument from partners. • The pretest is reviewed to confirm accuracy and appropriateness. • Preparation to administer the pretest to students has been planned, materials secured, and students and caregivers are notified. • Staff are able to score the pretest and assign students to working groups that have differing levels of competency represented.

Effective Implementation

Component	Quality Standards Questions	Suggestions	Indicators
Organization of Students into Study Groups	• Do staff have criteria and a process for organizing students into study groups or working groups?	• Identify options for grouping students and decide on a process that best suits the program goals and objectives. • Group students so that members of a group are at different competency levels yet within range of each other.	• Staff can explain the program's rationale for and the process used to organize students into groups. • Student work groups are diverse, using a number of different measures, e.g., school attended, grade and competency levels, etc.
Student and Family Orientation	Have the staff reflected on the potential of the opening year orientation and issues it might address, such as: • The mission and objectives of the program • Introduction of staff • Expectations and guidelines for behavior • Consequences for violation of program rules • Program activities and learning experiences • Ways for caregivers, family, and community to be involved.	• Involve staff in a reflection process regarding the potential to use the student–caregiver orientation to accomplish multiple goals. • Assign staff meaningful roles in the program. • Have additional program and registration materials available. • Collect student and caregiver feedback to indicate whether, and if so in which ways, the orientation was helpful.	• Staff are responsible for large segments of the orientation program. • Community members, caregivers, and students are part of the program. • The program is held in the community. • The program accomplishes multiple goals.
Planning for Opening Day	Has time has been allocated to plan for the first day of work with the students? Possible issues: • How will the day begin for students? • What is the protocol to be used by each staff member when working with students? • What will the staff do and say to set the tone desired for the day and the year?	• Work with staff to create a protocol or script for opening day. • Provide opportunities for staff to rehearse for opening day, with members playing roles of students and staff. • Structure time for feedback and improvement. • Review each staff member's materials for the first week. • Provide time to debrief from the first day.	• Staff can demonstrate how they will open their first day with students. • Materials have been reviewed, feedback provided, and suggestions implemented. • Staff workstations and/or rooms are ready for students. • Necessary calls have been made to students' homes for follow-up and/or welcome conversations.

171

Figure F.1. PI Rules and Series of Consequences

PROJECT INTERFACE

J. Alfred Smith Fellowship Hall
8500 "A" Street
Oakland, California 94621
(415) 635-1755

BASIC STUDENT RULES

These rules were developed with the thought, contributions, and effort of:

The Project Advisory Board
The Project Administrative & Tutorial Staff
The Project's Parent Club
Student Representatives

They represent the consensus of these members of the Project Interface Family as to rules that were most effective for us to abide by.

1. There will be no capping, casing, ranking, charging, or playing the dozens.
2. There will be no disrespect of fellow students, parents, or other adults.
3. Food is to be eaten *before* the project, during break, and after the project. This is a privilege that will be revoked if litter becomes a problem.
4. Students will bring necessary books and materials to the project each day. Students are to bring math books even when no homework has been assigned.
5. Students are expected to be diligent, try their hardest, and be consistent in studying outside of class.
6. There is to be *no* horseplay on the premises. This includes:
    running
    hitting
    wrestling
    hair-pulling
    tag
    taking others' belongings
    screaming
    not returning to your group promptly after break
7. There is to be no pencil sharpening or going to the restroom *except* during the break. Students are to use the free time available before the project and during break to take care of personal business.

If any of these rules are violated, the following series of consequences will go into effect:

STEP ONE: The student and the tutor will discuss the situation and hopefully resolve the problem.

STEP TWO: The student's parent will be called upon the very next infraction.

STEP THREE: The tutor, the director, and the student will meet.

STEP FOUR: A conference with the student, his/her parent(s), the tutor, and the director will be held.

- Students who destroy church property will have their parents called in.
- Parents will be asked to assume responsibility for the damages.

Figure F.2. Characteristics and Behaviors

This characteristics and behaviors chart contains some typical behaviors that came up in our program along with some suggested responses that we used effectively at Project Interface.

Some Characteristics and Behaviors shown by middle school students at Project Interface and suggested strategies for adults

Characteristics and Behaviors of Typically Developing Middle Schoolers	*Suggestions for Structure and Responses*
They talk all the time *Example:* I have seen children who literally cannot stop talking. They earnestly try very hard to stop, but they talk incessantly.	Tight structure and understanding are needed. • Teachers need a time and a firm commitment from the student to stop talking for specified lengths of time. • Rewards and consequences need to be agreed upon and supported by the parent or guardian. If the parent or guardian is ineffective, it may be necessary to identify adults in the child's life who can reinforce the program's efforts. • Engaging lessons that teach and/or incorporate things children want to learn can focus the direction of the talk. • Assignment of responsibilities and/or leadership tasks (especially when they have been earned) can be an effective reward. • Acknowledge effort and progress with a chart, table, or other visual aid.
They will not talk at all *Example:* I have had to sit silently for as long as 30 minutes before a child was able and/or willing to talk.	These first two examples are exceptions to the rule; most children lie somewhere in between these extremes. However, a significant amount of emotional and spiritual energy is required to work with these extremes on a daily basis. • Respect the silence and remain open. State boundaries, e.g., confidentiality, privacy, etc. • Make sure there is a clear understanding of expectations for behavior and work at the program. • In groups, assign a role that requires speaking. • Or leave them be, and let them come around.

(continued)

173

Figure F.2. (*continued*)

Characteristics and Behaviors of Typically Developing Middle Schoolers	Suggestions for Structure and Responses
They do not walk *Example:* They stroll, run, sashay, skip, pace, meander, and hop. They eventually get to where they are going, but they do not walk.	This has to be codified as a formal rule inside and outside, except on playing fields. Rigorously follow the series of consequences.
They are mentally quick and bright, but scattered *Example:* They will stop paying attention in the middle of a conversation, class, or activity. I have seen students genuinely forget books, clothing, and even their junk food.	Important things must be repeated regularly before a positive habit sinks in and takes effect. Learn to discern between the honest forgetfulness and the ploy (this can be difficult, but careful observation of eyes and body language can help). • Ask them to repeat what was said back to you. • Make sure they write down everything that is most important. • Teach them how to organize their schoolwork by subject and how to take notes. • Where lack of attention is deliberate or consistent, use the series of consequences. • Share your own difficulties and tips you have used. • Acknowledge and reward progress.
They can be relentless when engaged in a project they find interesting or challenging	This explains the length to which students will go for the right hairstyle or cut, regardless of the time involved; why they will play video games endlessly; and why they are frequently distracted in school.

Characteristics and Behaviors of Typically Developing Middle Schoolers	Suggestions for Structure and Responses
They will argue and ask "why" about everything Some of the reasons our students argued: • To kill time • To dissuade an adult from a course of action • To persuade an adult to a course of action • To test to see whether or not an adult would give in • To test their own reasoning ability—sometimes they were thinking out loud • To get attention • To win • To show disrespect for authority • To show regard that acknowledges a relationship	Explicit explanations that tell why, when, how, and where are necessary for even the obvious procedures and rules. Many explanations, which seem rational and acceptable to adults, are frequently rejected by students and dismissed without a second thought if at all possible. This can be especially true if the adult is a parent, teacher, or other authority figure. A sense of how they think can enable an adult to generate explanations that make sense to students, even if they would not make sense to other adults. • Patience and willingness to unpack, explain, and/or review even the basic rules are needed. When discussing requirements, necessary changes or actions, and assignments, offer the explanations and ask for questions. Unless there is an emergency or you are at that point in the series of consequences, rarely tell a student something without offering an explanation. • Once explanations have been clearly offered, it is important to be able to stand firm without buckling to whining, tears, anger, pouting, or more arguing. • Recognize the point at which discussion ceases, announce it, and begin to attend to the business at hand. • Fairness and firmness are essential. A fair adult does not display disdain, dismissal, or condescension when working through arguments with students. • A sense of humor helps in the generation of explanations that make sense to middle school students

(continued)

Figure F.2. *(continued)*

Characteristics and Behaviors of Typically Developing Middle Schoolers	*Suggestions for Structure and Responses*
They engage in outright defiance As with arguing, outright defiance can occur for many reasons, for example: • To test their own strength and power • To intimidate or bully • To cover fear and vulnerability • To get attention • To displace anger and aggression to a target they deem safe • To win • To show disrespect for authority • As a response to an organizational climate that lacks clearly enforced boundaries for behavior and allows inappropriate displays • As a response to actual or perceived unfairness • As a cry for help • As a response to an incident that is experienced by the student as "the straw that broke the camel's back" • As a symptom of untreated and/or unacknowledged abuse	Defiance is a highly provocative behavior. More than some other behaviors, it cannot be understood out of the context or situation in which it occurs. The causes of defiance can be difficult to discern and are sometimes complex and contradictory. While the causes do not condone or justify outright defiance, it is important to remember them when formulating a response to a child's behavior. Even the most effective adults will experience outright defiance at some point in their careers.
At times, they will show as much disrespect as they are allowed An example of this behavior occurred the first day Mrs. Johnson brought Joanne to Project Interface. The entire time that Mrs. Johnson and I talked, Joanne stood, with her hand on one hip and book bag in the other hand, looking upward, rolling her eyes, patting her foot, and making loud sighs at accurately chosen intervals. Joanne had clearly communicated to me that she did not want to be at a Project Interface, she came because she had no choice, she did not like it, and she did not intend to like it or me—all without saying a word.	I never had conversations with girls when they were rolling their necks with their hands on their hips and their feet in position for two reasons. First, it reeks of disrespect and is a stance that is not tolerated by many adults in the African American community. The child has to know that I know that this behavior is unacceptable in her community and that I will not tolerate it either. Second, the stance communicates that the child feels she is in a conversation with a peer and that she is just as "grown" as any adult woman—and certainly the one before whom she is standing.

Figure G.1. Use of Bloom's Stages of the Affective Domain to Develop Strategies to Engage and Motivate Students

Chapter 8 describes the importance of reaching children in order to engage them and the way we structured our program to build engagement and nurture students. Bloom's Taxonomy of the Affective Domain shows the levels of emotional attachment to the educational process that our students proceeded through and the goals that they attained. The left-hand column of the chart below shows the stages in Bloom's Taxonomy of the Affective Domain (Bloom, 1956). I have added two additional columns based on our experiences at PI. The middle column shows typical behaviors and attitudes that students may exhibit in relation to the corresponding affective domain, and the right-hand column shows suggestions for strategies to use in interaction with students at each stage.

Use of Bloom's Stages of the Affective Domain to Develop Strategies to Engage and Motivate Students

Bloom's Taxonomy of the Affective Domain	Typical Behaviors and Attitudes That Often Accompany Each Domain	Suggested Strategies That Can Reach, Motivate, and Engage Students at Each Domain
Introduction		
The Affective Domain The affective domain focuses on the student's emotional attachment to the educational process; it explores and explains the process through which student attitudes, interests, appreciation, and ability to change may be assessed. Accurate assessment of where a student is or seems to be on this continuum can be useful in designing and implementing strategies to facilitate the student's positive emotional engagement with school.	This list in this column is suggestive only; it is best used for reflection and for sharpening observation and interpretation skills. • Student behavior is complex and not always easily understood, interpreted, and responded to in ways that further the educative process. The complexity of student behavior is especially important to recognize in order to engage and connect with students who are in states one or two (low levels) of Bloom's Taxonomy. • The identical behavior can mean different things when coming from different students or the same student on a different day. • Students are masters at reading adults; many adults fail miserably when reading student behavior.	These strategies are suggestive and are best used when accompanied with reflection, observation, discussion, and the ability to examine one's practice in an objective manner to observe its effect on students. • Unfortunately, there is no silver bullet. There is no such thing as one way that always works with every student every day, and without knowing the context and the specifics of a given situation, it is very difficult for an observer to respond to the frequently asked, "What do you do when . . ." questions that many of us have. • Teaching is a complex, situational, and ever-changing exercise that requires consistent presence of mind and the ability to accurately interpret situations and respond proactively.

(continued)

Figure G.1. (continued)

Bloom's Taxonomy of the Affective Domain	Typical Behaviors and Attitudes That Often Accompany Each Domain	Suggested Strategies That Can Reach, Motivate, and Engage Students at Each Domain
1.0 The First Domain: RECEIVING (ATTENDING)		
The First Domain is concerned with: • The student's willingness to pay attention to classroom activity • Getting and holding the student's attention It consists of three subcategories that indicate three different levels of receptivity: **1.1. Awareness** The student is aware of the situation, phenomenon or problem he/she is confronting. **1.2. Willingness to Receive** The student is willing to notice the situation, etc., and give it his/her attention. **1.3.Controlled or Selected Attention** The student controls and focuses his/her attention, even when distractions are present.	Students centered in domain one are essentially shut down and turned off; they exhibit little, if any, engagement or effort and can be disruptive. At the first two stages, a student may have enrolled because a caregiver insisted, or the student thought that he/she wanted to enroll, but later experiences second thoughts and may exhibit some of these behaviors, characteristics, and attitudes: • Tardy • Absent frequently • Arrives without notebook and materials or books • Turns homework in rarely, or it is incomplete and incorrect • Hostile and defensive • Talks all of the time • Quiet and unobtrusive if left alone • They engage in off-task behavior during class and can carry a group away from the task at hand • They are usually bright • Their peers are all-important to them; they are loyal to a fault; they will not compete against each other in academic settings and will support one another, even when they are wrong and know that they are wrong.	**Establish a Connection and Lay the Foundation for Work to Begin** • Understand that the "work" with students in this domain is to create a relationship in which they are willing to consider what you are saying. • Identify as many areas of agreement as possible between you and the students. • Break the ice with an effort at humor, a story, or an anecdote in which you learned a lesson or were in an uncomfortable situation. Make contact with the students and their caregivers offline. Contact caregivers before class starts or shortly afterwards. • Act on the folk saying that many people "don't care what you know until they know that you care." Initiate conversations, communicate openly on the student's "turf"—at local churches, markets, or places you know students and their families frequent. • Communicate the fact that you realize your position is not the only solution or viewpoint. Communicate respect for and acknowledgment of their perspectives, feelings, and sense of integrity. At the same time, communicate the finer points and advantages of your position. • Avoid believing that you are logical, correct, and right. If students are to connect with you so that you will be able to teach them, they will have to be genuinely convinced that you have something to offer in terms that are meaningful to them. • Call on significant adults and caregivers in the students' network for reinforcement and support so that, at a minimum, compliance is obtained. Accept the reality that students' enjoyment will come later.

178

Bloom's Taxonomy of the Affective Domain	Typical Behaviors and Attitudes That Often Accompany Each Domain	Suggested Strategies That Can Reach, Motivate, and Engage Students at Each Domain
2.0 The Second Domain: RESPONDING		
The Second Domain is concerned with: Active participation on the part of the student; seeking out a subject or activity and attending to it **2.1. Acquiescence in responding** Acquiescence indicates passiveness on the student's part; compliance and obedience best describe the behavior and attitude here; the student does what he/she has been asked but has not really accepted the necessity for doing so. **2.2. Willingness to respond** Response with the required behavior is done voluntarily, as opposed to being insisted upon and the possibility of consequences. **2.3. Satisfaction in response** The student has gone beyond the previous level and now experiences satisfaction and a sense of personal fulfillment after having participated in learning experiences.	Most students did only what was necessary to get by and balked at requests for increased effort and increased rigor and quantity of schoolwork. Most of them had never really put forth genuine effort. A number of factors accounted for this lack of effort: • They react to extremely low expectations for their behavior and achievement by confirming them. • They stop trying as a psychological buffer against repeated failure. • They refuse to work "for" and with adults whom they experience as patronizing, condescending, or who appear not to care about them as people. • They successfully bluff, manipulate, or wear out adults who make efforts to get them to do more work or better work. • They believe that if they persist in uncooperative, rebellious behavior that they can get adults to trade compliance and apparent cooperation for lowered academic demands. • They are bored and/or turned off by the content of the work they are asked to do or the instructional strategies used in the learning experiences.	**Get Their Attention; Motivate; Engage and Encourage Students to Try** • Place and explain the work in terms of their frame of reference and what is important to them. Begin the introduction to class lessons by framing the work from case studies, examples, narratives, and stories with which the students are familiar and that have meaning to them. Lyrics from current songs, themes from television shows and films they watch, and issues currently pervasive in their community are all sources of information about students that can create a "hook" that will get students' attention long enough for them to begin to focus on the work. • Research on pop culture will pay off handsomely here because interesting data can be found, such as this statement made by Ice-T: "... kids from the ghetto need to learn how to be less aggressive and how to solve more of their problems with their brains...the skills they learn *on* the street are as valuable as the skills they learn *off* the street" (Ice-T & Siegmund, 1994). • Ask for small, incremental steps that can be documented and are challenging yet doable. • Continue to break the work into manageable pieces. Do not assign a term paper; assign each phase of the research and writing process. • Point out incremental progress and encourage students to build on it. • Keep standards high and be consistent with consequences. • Demonstrate that you can understand both sides of an issue; stress win–win, not win–lose. • Stress and be able to demonstrate in terms that are real to students the connection between your work and their interests and aspirations. • Stress mutual benefits and losses if students balk at working harder on difficult work. • Describe in graphic terms, using metaphors they can relate to, how much better things could be if they work with you instead of against you. The improvements stated should be short-term and long-term situations. • Create a strategy to win over or neutralize influential disruptive students. • Follow-up with students and caregivers online and offline.

(continued)

179

Figure G.1. (conintued)

Bloom's Taxonomy of the Affective Domain	Typical Behaviors and Attitudes That Often Accompany Each Domain	Suggested Strategies That Can Reach, Motivate, and Engage Students at Each Domain
3.0 The Third Domain: VALUING		
The Third Domain is concerned with: • The value a student places upon a particular object or behavior • The value is a social product that has been slowly internalized and accepted, and is now used by the student based on his/her own criteria of worth • Behavior characterized by valuing is motivated by the individual's commitment to the underlying value that guides the overt behavior **3.1. Acceptance of a Value** There is a consistency of response so that others perceive the student as holding the belief or value. At this level, the student is willing to be identified as such, e.g., "I am an Interface student; that means . . ." **3.2. Preference for a Value** Behavior at this level implies not merely the acceptance of a value to the point of being willing to be identified with it, but the student is committed enough to pursue it, seek it, and desire it. **3.3. Commitment** Commitment involves a high degree of certainty and conviction. A firm emotional acceptance of a belief and a loyalty to a group, position, or cause are present. The student acts to further the school or program in some way; he/she tries to convince others of the validity of his cause.	At this stage the student's attitude begins to shift significantly so that the student assumes active control of behavior, assumes responsibility for effort, and becomes proactive in pursuit of goals that have now been internalized and are experienced by the student as his/her own values or as shared values, not simply the program's goals. • Valuing behavior is not motivated by the desire to comply or the need to obey, but by the student's commitment to the underlying values that guide behavior. • Even though the abstract concept of the intrinsic worth of something is the result of the student's own internal process, • the process of coming to value a new idea results from the context or environment a student experiences, and • the internal valuing process is influenced by social interaction with others.	Motivate and Set High, Reasonable, and Feasible Goals • Encourage and invite questions and further clarification. State that you are prepared to make it as clear as they need it, and be willing to review, restate, and repeat in as many different ways as needed. • Be clear on exactly what it is they have do—provide an example of what is expected and what is not acceptable. Review the examples thoroughly and explain why one is better than the other. • Offer clear, constructive criticism with praise for specific accomplishments, e.g., notebook is in better shape, sentences are more complex, tardiness has decreased. Do not offer general praise such as "You're a good guy." • Encourage them to stretch, take risks; assure them that risks are necessary, appropriate, and that you will be there to help them. • Stress that more is always required for movement and success. • Encourage them to rise to the occasion and show that they are serious or at least putting forth real effort. • Stay in touch with caregivers and other adults who provide reinforcement and encouragement to students. • Acknowledge and reward student effort, success, progress, and engagement, particularly their first B, good test and report card grades, and other markers of improved academic achievement.

180

Bloom's Taxonomy of the Affective Domain	Typical Behaviors and Attitudes That Often Accompany Each Domain	Suggested Strategies That Can Reach, Motivate, and Engage Students at Each Domain

4.0 The Fourth Domain: ORGANIZATION

The Fourth Domain is concerned with: Bringing together different values, resolving conflicts among them, and establishing the most important ones that will serve as guides for beliefs and actions	The student is working on emotional and mental levels here. He/she is bringing together a complex set of values, resolving conflicts, and beginning to build an internally consistent system where he/she can be an achiever, be "cool," go to college, and be with his/her "homies."	Continue Motivation and Support Their Beliefs and Values
4.1. Conceptualization of a value	He/she sees how the new values relate to those he/she has held onto; if he/she can mimic the walk of the dudes on the street, he/she can also ask for help in filling out a financial aid application. If he/she knows his/her grandmother prays for his/her safety, he/she can also ask her to pray that he/she passes his/her exams and gets into college.	• Ask for clear, definite actions on the student's part. Make sure they know what to do and how to do it. Ask them to show, tell, and/or explain to you how, what, and why they plan to accomplish tasks and goals. • Make sure that they begin to move ahead as soon and as quickly as possible.
4.2. Organization of a value system A unity of beliefs, ideas, attitudes, and values has been made.	This synthesis and integration of new and old ways is not always easy or smooth, and the student can be in danger of a slip, or regression into old ways of thinking and acting. These can be opportunities for growth and renewed commitment or become steps that are so slippery, he/she cannot regain his grip on the new ways.	• Reinforce, nurture, and uphold their commitment and effort with affirming testimonials, ceremonies, and examples of the good results their peers have gotten from increased efforts. • Assure them that they can achieve these same results. • Stress identity and belonging to a group of achievers and strivers. • Encourage a sense of belonging to one another, e.g., their study group, the cause (doing well in school), and the larger group (Project Interface). • Prepare the students for encounters with others who will be hostile toward them. Teach them what to expect from their uncommitted peers and how to work with adults and authority figures who doubt their abilities.

(continued)

Bloom's Taxonomy of the Affective Domain	Typical Behaviors and Attitudes That Often Accompany Each Domain	Suggested Strategies That Can Reach, Motivate, and Engage Students at Each Domain
5.0 The Fifth Domain: CHARACTERIZATION BY A VALUE OR VALUE COMPLEX		

Bloom's Taxonomy of the Affective Domain	Typical Behaviors and Attitudes That Often Accompany Each Domain	Suggested Strategies That Can Reach, Motivate, and Engage Students at Each Domain
Characterization by a value or value complex is attained when: The student has a value system that has controlled his/her behavior such that he/she has developed a lifestyle as a successful student, and his/her behavior is pervasive, consistent, and predictable **5.1. Generalized set** A generalized set is a basic orientation that enables the student to reduce and order the multiple demands on him/her and to respond consistently and effectively. **5.2 Characterization** Characterization is the highest level of the internalization process where the student has synthesized beliefs and attitudes about being successful in school to the point where academic achievement, along with the attitudes, values, behaviors, and practices needed to achieve at or above grade level, are now the prevailing and determining frame of reference for the student.	The new values and behaviors have controlled and determined the student's behavior long enough to have become a way of life: • His/her behavior is pervasive, consistent, and predictable. • He/she has personally experienced the results of new study habits, study skills, self-confidence, effort, and engagement. • He/she has tasted success and realizes that it is not only possible but also doable. • This student is capable of helping new students with their own transitions and has become a full-fledged member of the program. This is the end result of program context and staff, caregivers, and teachers all working to create an environment that helps students through the transitions necessary to become an excellent student.	**Assist Students with Further Challenges** • Invite students to encourage one another and to discuss their successes and failures, along with positive feelings about their progress, schooling, and pursuit of an education. • Look for ways to encourage them to identify and work on their weak areas. • As they meet and achieve stated goals, help them to set new ones that continue to make them stretch and grow. Do not allow them to rest on their laurels. • Encourage them to support students who are not as far along as they are; ask them to see themselves as role models for younger students, and encourage them to show struggling and younger students how to accomplish what they have done. • Help them think about and begin to develop long-range plans for the big picture; give them broad outlines of the operational, incremental steps to their big aspirations and dreams. • Prepare them for setbacks, disappointment, perseverance, and even failure, along with much more hard work. • Help them to understand and accept that it will be as challenging for them as for anyone else, and possibly more so.

182

Figure H.1. Phases of Relationship Development with Caregivers

The following chart explains in detail the approach that we used for work with parents and caregivers.

Phase One: Earning Credibility and Endorsement

Issues Involved	Developing a Program That Meets Parental Expectations	Evidence of Effective Implementation
Acknowledgment of the implications of: • The way the larger society typically depicts poor people and/or the way it depicts people and communities of color • Personal perceptions, attitudes, and beliefs held by individual staff members about the children and families the program serves • The professional training and information most educators and social services professionals have received, and whether or not it prepared them adequately for effective work in poor communities • The role that the educational community has had in contributing to the estrangement between schools and poor children, families, and communities, and the lack of mutually supportive relationships with families and the immediate community.	1. Communicate beliefs, values, and corresponding program elements intentionally and explicitly to parents/caregivers to demonstrate that: • They will receive an honest, open hearing, without defensiveness, when they express concerns, perceptions, and opinions. • The program director is willing and able to facilitate communication between parents/caregivers and program staff. • The program director and staff are comfortable with them and their children, and family members and are willing to talk with them directly and honestly. • The program director is knowledgeable about the community's *strengths and resources*, as well its problems, and is able to coach the staff accordingly. • The program has their child's best interests at heart and genuinely holds high expectations for behavior and achievement of the program's goals (especially true for academic goals if the program has schoolwork or homework as a core component). • The program will provide high-quality services and learning activities that will enrich and strengthen the child's education, effort, and achievement. • The program acknowledges, appreciates, and understands their present involvement in the child's life.	• Parents/caregivers express comfort and engage in conversations about the program's goals; their children are open with one another and the program staff. • Explicit nonverbal communication indicates support for and agreement with program goals, guidelines, and activities. • Follow-through and responsiveness are demonstrated in returning and/or submitting documents and/or materials requested by the program. • Written feedback indicates and shares their level of enjoyment; comfort with and desire to endorse the program and concede to the program director's and staff's authority.

(continued)

Figure H.1. (*continued*)

Developing a Program That Meets Parental Expectations	Evidence of Effective Implementation
• The program realizes that a lack of involvement with, absence from, or participation in program activities does not necessarily indicate a lack of involvement with their child or concern about their academic success and overall well-being.	

2. Provide staff training on:
  • The program goals, standards, requirements, guidelines, expectations, activities, and learning experiences
  • Establishment of relationships with parents/caregivers as a necessary framework for student comfort, buy-in, and retention
  • Community resources and potential allies
	• Staff can share and discuss the goals, standards, requirements, guidelines, expectations, activities, and learning experiences with parents/caregivers.
	• Program staff assigned a specific group of children have personally made initial contact with each parent/caregiver so that the *first* contact and/or communication with a parent/caregiver is informative, inviting, encouraging, and positive.

3. Provide time for staff to reflect on, process, and discuss the implications of the way the larger society typically describes and discusses the people and community served and their own—perhaps unstated or even unacknowledged—biases and perceptions.	• Program staff accept the reality that building relationships with parents/caregivers and families is everyone's task, not solely the responsibility of the director or community resource person, and are able to draw from community resources.
4. Provide opportunities for staff to hear from and listen to parents and community members on issues directly related to program goals, activities, and learning experiences.	• Staff demonstrate high expectations by being prepared, aware of community mores, and able to state clear expectations for themselves and the children with whom they work.

184

Phase Two: Securing Continuity Between the Home and the Program

Issues Involved	Developing a Program That Meets Parental Expectations	Evidence of Effective Implementation

• Translating parent or caregiver endorsement into action
• Maintaining communication with parents/caregivers
• Providing an opportunity for the child to choose both the program and home, because they are in tandem with one another, instead of forcing a choice between the two
• Helping parents understand and realize the power and impact of what they do at home to affirm achievement and engagement at school, in spite of everything the child says to the contrary
• Supporting parents in the maintenance of high standards at home
• Parents often do not know specifically and strategically what to do, why they should do it, when and how to provide reinforcement at home
• Successful completion of the work required in Phase One, without which, educators *will not* be able to effectively provide strategies, tasks, and activities that constitute genuine involvement
	1. Explain to parents and review program activities, components, and structure, and explain why they are chosen; how they will directly benefit the child's development, academic achievement, and engagement in school; and how they will lead to long-term success.
	    The explanations have to be in words and language that parents/caregivers understand; any professional jargon, names, and terms (e.g., standardized tests and their scores, leveling) have to be fully unpacked and explained. An acknowledgment that professionals in any field make it difficult to communicate with anyone outside the field can also be helpful.
	2. Make sure the tasks asked of parents/caregivers can be done by any caring adult in the child's extended family network of biological and "fictive kin."
	3. Explain to parents the program rules, consequences, and the reasons for them.
	4. Explain to parents how your program measures whether or not students improve academically, and how the tasks you are requesting of them directly relate to their children's success.
	5. Make student involvement, effort, and success the focal point of all parent/caregiver meetings throughout the year.
		• Feedback from on-site participants indicates comfort with the orientation, scheduling, and experience of participating in on-site activities
		• Parent/caregiver volunteers refer friends to serve on-site
		• Parent/caregiver volunteers become repeat participants, and feel a connection to the program shown in ways such as:
		  • They ask if there are other ways they might support the project.
		  • They provide resources and materials.
		  • They refer friends.
		  • They contribute time and money.
		  • Students comment positively on parent volunteer contributions, especially reports that the volunteer inspired them, motivated them, or made them think.
		  • Staff express appreciation for the caregiver/volunteer contributions and increased awareness of the value of mutually supportive working relationships with parents and other caregivers.

(*continued*)

185

Figure H.I. (*continued*)

Phase Three: On-Site Involvement in the Work and Life of the Program

Issues Involved	Parental Expectations of the Program and Related Tasks	Evidence of Effective Implementation
• Structuring of tasks so that parents/caregivers see them as doable • Clarity on which tasks require training and which do not • Making the effort to match parental interests and skills with tasks that need to be done • Developing a broad base of involvement	1. Ask staff to identify ways they include caregivers and community members in the activities and learning experiences with students. It is important that staff can explain to parents/caregivers *why* they are doing a specific task or activity and *how* it contributes student engagement and achievement or the well-being and effectiveness of the program. Parents and caregivers need time to consider the frequency, hours, and days needed. Parent/caregiver volunteers can be effective in the following roles: • Guest speakers: sharing their life experiences, information about careers and education, or information on topics of interest identified by students. • Providing support for daily activities • Special skills and talents • Helping with major tasks or events 2. Provide parents/volunteers with a packet on the program and ways that individuals can contribute to the program. *(continued on next page)*	• Parents/caregivers feel comfortable and stop in for informal, unscheduled moments to observe their children or work on a project or activity. • Parents/caregivers recruit other parents. • Parents/caregivers attend activities designed especially for them. • Parents/caregivers make suggestions and express the feeling that they are heard and responded to by staff. • Parents/caregivers serve on formal committees. • Informal interactions between staff and parents or caregivers are a normal part of the day-to-day life of the project.

186

Parental Expectations of the Program and Related Tasks (*continued*)

3. Develop a form that asks parents/caregivers:
   - Which of the identified tasks listed would they be interested in doing
   - Their interests, if not listed
   - Best time to contact them
   - Days, hours, frequency they are available
   - Organizations to which they belong
   - Whether they would be comfortable sharing the program with their organization(s) and, if appropriate, solicit their involvement in the program
   - Whether they would serve as a volunteer coordinator and be willing to be trained to do this task

4. After the responses have been analyzed, ask the volunteer coordinator(s) to contact parent volunteers to:
   - Confirm interest and review responsibilities
   - Set up training time
   - Work with you and/or a staff member to develop a roster that outlines each task, the responsibilities, and the days and hours required
   - Participate in the design a volunteer orientation

5. Produce a grid, wall calendar, bulletin board, or some other means of posting volunteers for the day, week, and month for use by staff and volunteers.

6. Provide acknowledgment for volunteers: Events, certificates, or photographs are all appropriate.

References

Bennet, G. W. (1983). *Effective urban church ministry.* Nashville: Broadman Press.

Billingsley, A. (1992). *The Black family in White America* (2nd ed.). New York: Simon & Schuster.

Bloom, B. S. (1956). *Taxonomy of educational objectives, Handbook I: The cognitive domain.* New York: David McKay.

California State Board of Education. (1983). *Raising expectations: Model graduation requirements.* Sacramento: Author.

Clewell, B. C., Anderson, B. T., & Thorpe, M. E. (1992). *Breaking the barriers: Helping female and minority students succeed in mathematics and science.* San Francisco: Jossey-Bass.

Frye, H. et al. (1989, August). *Making the future different: Models of community intervention for academic achievement among African American youth in California,* Vol. II. Berkeley: University of California.

Ice-T, & Siegmund, H. (1994). *Ice opinion.* New York: St Martin's Press.

Lewis, O. (1961). *The children of Sanchez: Autobiography of a Mexican family* (3rd ed.). New York: Random House.

Marshall, J., Jr. (1996). *Street soldier.* New York: Delacorte Press.

National Commission on Excellence in Education. (1983). *A nation at risk: A report to the nation and the secretary of education.* Washington, DC: U.S. Government Printing Office.

Office of Policy Planning and Research. (1965). *The Negro family: The case for national action.* Washington, DC: United States Department of Labor.

Ozretich, R., & Bowman, S. R. (2001). *Middle childhood and adolescent development* [EC 1527]. Retrieved March 30, 2006, from http://eesc.orst.edu/agcomwebfile/edmat/ec1527.pdf

Pearson, W., Jr., & Bechtel, H. K. (Eds.). (1989). *Blacks, science, and American education.* New Brunswick, NJ: Rutgers University Press.

Peters, T. (1982). *In search of excellence.* New York: Harper & Row.

Silberman, C. (1964). *Crisis in Black and White.* New York: Random House.

University of California. (1989a). *Making the future different: Models of community intervention for academic achievement among African-American youth in California* (Vol. 1). Oakland: University of California Press.

University of California. (1989b). *Making the future different: Models of community intervention for academic achievement among African-American youth in California* (Vol. 2). Oakland: University of California Press.

Utah State Office of Education. *Mathematics, engineering, science achievement.* Retrieved March 30, 2006, from www.usoe.k12.ut.us/curr/MESA/default.htm

Index

About the Author

ANNE BOUIE works with policy makers and practitioners to design and implement processes and programs that result in positive change in school systems, schools, and classrooms. These learning experiences help clients learn and adopt habits of mind and effective practices that enhance teacher autonomy, their sense of efficacy in the classroom, and ability to work as members of an adult learning community. This work with administrators and policy makers is designed to create contexts and foster practices that create positive learning environments for staff and students. This process work is employed in these content areas:

- Raising student academic achievement
- Establishing and maintaining mutually supportive relationships with parents, families, and communities
- Designing and implementing supplementary and after-school enrichment programs for students
- Designing new teacher induction programs and ongoing professional development programs for experienced teachers

Since 1992, Dr. Bouie has worked in school systems across the country and with organizations whose mission is to bring positive change to urban schools. She has written and implemented professional development plans for site and central office staff and administrators in Philadelphia's public schools, utilized in other schools districts as well. A fellowship at The Department of Education's Office of Research and Improvement provided an opportunity to design and implement an exploratory study on the relationship of teacher habits of mind to student achievement. She has evaluated the results of in-school study groups on teacher habits of mind and classroom practices, and collected data to observe and chronicle the development of beginning teachers over time which will be used in future writing and research.

Dr. Bouie holds a Ph.D. in Policy Administration and Analysis, an M.A. in Secondary Education, and an M.A. in African and African–American history, all earned from Stanford University.